CW01668396

A Beginner's Guide to Special Makeup Effects

A Beginner's Guide to Special Makeup Effects: Monsters, Maniacs and More is an introduction to special effects makeup using cost-effective tools and materials that can be found in local stores.

The book is divided into three sections – Simple Makeup, Advanced Materials and Techniques and Advanced Makeup – and features tutorials to create characters such as a pirate, vampire, ghost, robot, burn victim, witch, zombie and goblin. Each character is introduced with a full-page photograph of the finished makeup and illustrated with full-color, step-by-step photographs. The book also includes instructions on how to make fake teeth, apply bald caps, create gory wounds and injuries and make simple prosthetics. Each makeup tutorial is designed to progressively build on the techniques outlined in the preceding tutorial, guiding readers from the basics of foundation, highlight and shadow to creating advanced creature makeups.

This is a beginner makeup book suited for students of Stage Makeup courses, as well as for the theatre technician working and training on their own.

Christopher Payne has been a professional makeup artist for more than 15 years and an enthusiastic amateur for most of his life before that. He has an MFA in Makeup and Wig Design from the University of Cincinnati and has worked on theatrical productions, television shows and films across the country. He has also taught makeup at a number of schools, trade shows and theaters. This is Payne's second book project, having previously contributed to Makeup Artistry for Film and Television (Sciortino, 2021).

A Beginner's Guide to Special Makeup Effects

Monsters, Maniacs and More

Christopher Payne
with photography by Andrew Kjos

Routledge
Taylor & Francis Group
NEW YORK AND LONDON

First published 2021
by Routledge
52 Vanderbilt Avenue, New York, NY 10017

and by Routledge
2 Park Square, Milton Park, Abingdon, Oxon, OX14 4RN

Routledge is an imprint of the Taylor & Francis Group, an informa business

Library of Congress Cataloging-in-Publication Data
Names: Payne, Christopher, (Makeup artist) author.
Title: A beginner's guide to special makeup effects : monsters, maniacs and more / Christopher Payne ; with photography by Andrew Kjos
Description: New York : Routledge, 2021. | Includes index.
Identifiers: LCCN 2020034350 (print) | LCCN 2020034351 (ebook) | ISBN 9780367554668 (hardback) | ISBN 9780367554675 (paperback) | ISBN 9781003093701 (ebook)
Subjects: LCSH: Theatrical makeup—Handbooks, manuals, etc. | Theatrical prosthetic makeup—Handbooks, manuals, etc.
Classification: LCC PN2068 .P37 2021 (print) | LCC PN2068 (ebook) | DDC 792.02/7—dc23
LC record available at https://lccn.loc.gov/2020034350
LC ebook record available at https://lccn.loc.gov/2020034351

ISBN: 978-0-367-55466-8 (hbk)
ISBN: 978-0-367-55467-5 (pbk)
ISBN: 978-1-003-09370-1 (ebk)

Typeset in Gill Sans
by Apex CoVantage, LLC

For Dick, Stan, Rick and Rob

Without whom I'd probably be
spending my life in a cubicle

CONTENTS

SECTION 2: ADVANCED MATERIALS AND TECHNIQUES

SECTION 3: ADVANCED MAKEUP

INTRODUCTION

PREFACE

I grew up with a passion for movies, and for movie monsters. I was never much of a horror fan, but boy howdy was I a science fiction and fantasy nerd. *The Terminator, Predator, Robocop, Batman, Teenage Mutant Ninja Turtles* and, of course, *Star Trek* and *Star Wars*. Throw into the mix the fact that my family has been heavily involved in community theater for several generations and you can literally say I was raised on this stuff. When Arnold got shot up in *T2*, revealing the robot underneath, I just had to try it on myself with tinfoil and latex. The results were . . . less than spectacular. But that passion to experiment, play and create was born. For better or worse, I was a makeup artist from that point on.

Of course, this was all during the dark ages before the internet was a thing. For a kid trying to do makeup in the little studio his parents let him set up in the laundry room, information was tough to come by. There were a few theater makeup books that I could check out from the library, but for me the holy grail was *Dick Smith's Monster Makeup Handbook*. My parents bought me a copy and I devoured that thing, trying every makeup in its hallowed pages. I still have it, the pages covered in nose putty and stuck together with spirit gum.

Flash forward a couple decades, I'd somehow found myself living the dream: I was a real-life, professional makeup artist. Along the way I also found a passion for education and had taught at several schools, theaters and conventions around the country. Makeup books were becoming much more common than when I was growing up, but I felt they also tended to get advanced pretty quickly. Many of them have a few basic makeups before you're sculpting, making molds and spending big bucks on professional-grade materials and equipment. I felt a need for someone just getting started, which is where the seeds for this book began to germinate. The idea was simple: write a book in which a costume shop and a few other local stores are all the reader needs to start making monsters.

It took a lot of years and a lot of effort to get this book into your hands, more than I ever would have imagined when I first started.

In the beginning, I had the idea that the book would appeal mostly to kids, so that's who I used as my models in the first draft. I got about a quarter of the way into it before I started showing the rough draft to people for feedback. The response I got was pretty universal: people thought they were cute facepaints on adorable youngsters, then set the draft aside without much more thought. Clearly, I had miscalculated and would need to try again.

My second attempt used older models, and again, after I got about a quarter of the way into it, I had a few people take a look to get feedback. This time the problem was one that I could see for myself: the photography. Regardless of the quality of my makeup, I was an amateur photographer with a hobby-grade camera, and it really showed. If this book was going to be a reality, I needed to get serious about the photos.

Enter Andrew Kjos. I met Andrew on a social media forum for photographers, models and makeup artists. He was intrigued by the idea and agreed to take the pictures. Not only did he take the studio shots of all the different steps and the final makeups, but he also took in-progress shots that I didn't even realize I needed until I started putting the book together and thinking, "thank goodness he got a shot of me doing that." Andrew is responsible for most of the photographs in this book and is a big part of why it looks as good as it does.

Finally, the book was complete, but I still had no publisher. I spent a long time researching and reaching out, trying to wrap my brain around the world of book publication and literary agents, before a couple friends who were published with Routledge told me to reach out to that company. Ironically, Routledge was the one publisher I had never contacted because they deal mainly in textbooks, which I had never considered my book to be. They thought otherwise, luckily for me.

I want to thank a handful of people who helped me to make this book. Andrew for his beautiful photography. Jake, Ingrid, Dan, Zoë, Misael and Jessica for letting me glue stuff to their faces. Daniel Townsend and Christine Sciortino for pointing me in the right direction when I was looking for a publisher, and editors Stacey Walker, Lucia Accorsi and Laurie Fuller for holding my hand and baby walking me through the submission and publication process. Kelly Yurko for both being my teacher back in school and my proofreader for this book. And everyone who gave me feedback on various drafts over the years.

With the basics covered in this book, I'd love to write a sequel getting into more advanced makeups and techniques. A surprising number of costume and Halloween stores are starting to carry foam latex prosthetics, alcohol-based makeup and other really cool stuff. If that's something you'd be interested in, give Routledge a shout and let them know. For now, have fun getting your hands dirty and jumping into the amazing world of special makeup effects. If you're anything like me, you're going to have a great time.

Christopher Payne

TOOLS AND MATERIALS

Here are some of the things that you will use as you create the characters in this book:

MAKEUP

The most basic material that you will use is . . . makeup! There are several kinds of makeup available in most costume shops and drugstores.

Cream Makeup

Cream makeup has an oil base and a creamy texture, hence the name. It's available in just about any color you can imagine, and you can easily mix different colors together to create even more variety. Because cream makeup has oil in it, you have to set it with powder to keep it from smearing. I personally prefer this kind of makeup and have used it for all of the characters in this book.

Cake Makeup

Cake makeup is a powdered product that has been pressed into a container, resulting in a hard disc. It's activated with water, usually using a damp sponge or brush. If you use less water you get less makeup, but it's easier to control on your face. More water means more makeup, but it's harder to control. Cake makeup involves a bit of a learning curve, but it provides vibrant colors and fast application (really handy if you're doing body makeup!). Cake makeup does not need to be powdered; once it's dry, the stuff is fairly smudgeproof, *until* you splash water on it – then your whole makeup will turn into a runny mess.

Pressed Powders

Pressed powders are similar to cake makeup but are meant to be applied dry with a fluffy brush. Eyeshadow is an example of a pressed powder, but it doesn't have to be used on just the eyes! This is a good product to use to create skin texture and contouring. You can build it up gradually until you have the intensity you want.

Liquid Makeup

Liquid makeup is . . . well . . . liquid makeup. It's typically water or silicone-based, and is sold in a variety of colors. Drugstores carry most skin tones in their makeup section, and costume shops carry other colors. Liquid makeup is usually used for the foundation layer, and then other products are used on top. Like cream makeup, liquid makeup should be powdered once it has dried.

ADHESIVE

Adhesive is a fancy term for glue. Don't just grab any old glue, though! I've heard horror stories of people trying to use superglue to attach something to their face and then needed an emergency room visit to get it back off. There are several types of adhesive that are designed to be used on your skin:

Spirit Gum

This is the most commonly available makeup adhesive. It's often used in theater, in haunted houses and on Halloween. You remove it with spirit gum remover or rubbing alcohol.

You can buy spirit gum at any costume shop, and practically everywhere around Halloween. The other adhesives listed below may have to be purchased online, though bigger costume shops may carry them.

Acrylic Adhesive

The most popular form of acrylic adhesive is called Pros-Aide, though there are other versions with different names. It's a contact adhesive, which means that you get the strongest bond when you paint two surfaces (like your skin and the inside of a fake nose), let them dry and then press the two surfaces together. Pros-Aide requires a special remover, the two most common being Pros-Aide Remover and isopropyl myristate.

Silicone Adhesive

Silicone-based adhesives are very strong and are one of the more popular options used by professionals. They can be used for any makeup that needs a really strong hold. The downside to silicone adhesive is the price: at the time of this writing, you can buy nearly eight bottles of spirit gum for the cost of one bottle of silicone adhesive.

BALD CAPS

Bald caps are coverings for your head that make you look bald. They come in a variety of materials such as rubber, vinyl and plastic. Costume shops usually carry rubber caps, sometimes in different sizes (though cheaper ones tend to be "one size fits all").

BLOOD

Fake blood (also called stage blood) is essential to any good horror makeup. Many companies have their own versions of it, but you can also make your own. There are a few recipes for homemade blood in this book, and there are dozens (maybe hundreds) more that you can find online.

If you're planning on using store-bought blood in your mouth, make sure it's meant for that. Some bloods contain chemicals that make it look and flow more realisitcally, but aren't safe to ingest. Any blood designed to be safe to put in your mouth will say so right on the label.

BRUSHES

Brushes are one of the main tools for applying makeup. They come in all shapes and sizes. You don't need the best of the best to learn with, though. Many drugstores sell packages of inexpensive makeup brushes. When I was first learning to do makeup, most of my brushes came from the local craft store and worked just fine! I got some weird looks in the brush aisle, testing each one against my face to find ones whose bristles were silky to the touch yet still firm.

COLLODION

Non-flexible collodion (also called rigid collodion) is an ether or acetone-based liquid plastic that is used to create a variety of wound effects. It shrinks slightly when it dries, causing the skin to pucker and contract.

CREPE WOOL

Crepe wool (also called crepe hair) is used to create fake beards, animal fur and other hairy details. It's sold in tight braids and is available in a variety of colors that can be used on their own or mixed to create a custom color blend.

GELATIN

Gelatin is used to create burn makeups and funky skin textures. You can purchase it at the supermarket, but make sure you get the unflavored kind. Knox is the most common brand, and it's sold in handy little packets so you can make a little bit at a time. Gelatin is also available premade from special effects suppliers, typically in slabs or cubes.

GLYCERIN

Glycerin is a clear liquid available in most drugstores. It's pretty handy for creating sweat and other shines and can be used as a component in gelatin.

HAIR COLOR

Spray-in hair color is very useful for creating a character when you don't want to use a wig. Most costume shops carry it, and it washes out in the shower.

HAIR GEL AND HAIR SPRAY

You will use hair gel and hair spray to complete your character for several of the makeups in this book, but you don't need the best of the best. The cheap stuff works just fine.

LIQUID LATEX

Liquid latex is a liquid rubber product that is used for many makeup applications, from skin textures to larger buildups. It contains ammonia to keep it liquid and dries as the ammonia evaporates.

Latex eyelash adhesive (such as Duo) is a thicker form of liquid latex with very little ammonia in it. It's a safer product to use near your eyes, as there won't be any ammonia fumes to irritate them (this can be a hazard with liquid latex).

Most people are fine using liquid latex on their skin, but some people have a latex allergy. If you're not sure, try applying a drip to the inside of your wrist. If you're fine after a few hours, great. If you have an allergy, your skin will get red and itchy. If that's the case, skip the makeups in this book that use latex (or do them on someone else while wearing latex-free gloves).

MAKEUP PENCILS

Makeup pencils are sold at any costume shop or drugstore and can be used for details such as eyebrows and veins and on other occasions where lines are needed. Many of them specify that they're either for the eyes or the lips, but you can use them anywhere on your face. Eye pencils tend to be a little harder than lip pencils.

Be sure to buy a sharpener to keep a fine point on your pencils. Not any pencil sharpener will do; get one made for makeup pencils.

POWDER

Makeup setting powder is used on cream and liquid makeup to keep it from smearing. It comes in a variety of colors, but you typically want to use translucent powder (powder without any color added). This will set your makeup without changing the color.

POWDER PUFF

A powder puff is a soft fabric disc that's designed to hold powder as you're setting makeup. They're available in a variety of sizes, but bigger ones are easier to work with. When they get dirty, you can toss them into the laundry and resuse them when they're clean! They're also cheap enough to throw away after each use if you prefer.

PROSTHETICS

A prosthetic, also called an appliance, is any premade item that you glue to your skin as part of a makeup. Costume shops usually sell basic noses, horns and other small items, and some are starting to carry higher-quality foam latex and even silicone options. I'll show you how to make some simple prosthetics in this book.

PUTTY AND WAX

Nose putty and mortician's wax are among the oldest special effects materials and were responsible for some of the most iconic movie monsters in Hollywood's golden age.

They are considered pretty old-school these days and are not really used much professionally anymore, but for cheap learning materials that are available locally they can't be beat.

RUBBER MASK GREASEPAINT

Rubber mask greasepaint (also called RMG) is a special kind of cream makeup made to be used on latex makeup. If you use ordinary cream makeup on latex, the rubber will slowly absorb the oil in the makeup, causing the whole thing to discolor (usually it goes sort of gray). RMG has a heavy castor oil base, so it has more than enough to keep the makeup from discoloring on latex.

SPATULAS

Small spatulas are available at beauty supply stores; you can use them to scoop out makeup onto a clean palette in order to keep everything hygenic.

SPONGES

Sponges are an alternative to brushes when applying makeup. Triangular wedge sponges are the most common variety and are available in both latex and non-latex forms. They can be used smooth or with the end torn off for more textured effects.

Natural sea sponges are also used for applying cake makeup, especially when you have to cover a large area. They are also useful for dabbing on makeup to create texture effects.

Stipple sponges have a coarse texture and are used to create scratches, stubble and other textures.

THERMOPLASTIC

Thermoplastic is a type of plastic that melts at a very low temperature. It's available in both pellets and sheets, and you can use it to create fangs, dentures, claws, horns and a variety of other things. It's very useful stuff! The brand I've found most often is called Friendly Plastic, though there are others out there.

TOOTH ENAMEL

Tooth enamel is a paint-on product to change the color of your teeth. It comes in black, nicotine, gold, rotten green and a variety of other colors. You can easily remove it by brushing your teeth.

MEET THE MODELS

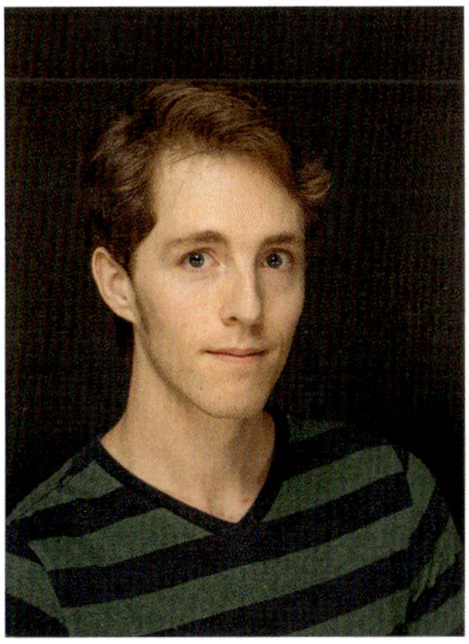

Jake Miser

Ingrid Burton

Dan Royce

Zoë Morse-Brown

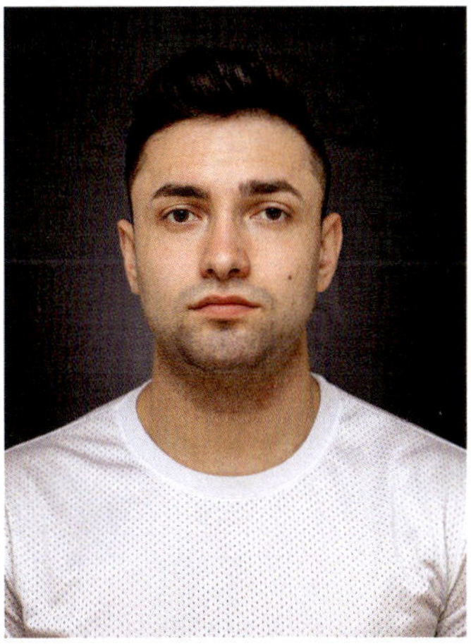

Misael Miranda

Jessica Cook

SECTION I

SIMPLE MAKEUP

CHAPTER 1
PIRATE

A **pirate** is a great introduction to some basic makeup concepts, and you can have a lot of creative fun with the details. Some things that most pirates seem to have in common are bad skin, sunburn, scars and stubble. The more disgusting you make this character, the better it will look. When the makeup is done, you can add a clip-on earring, eye patch and wig to finish the look.

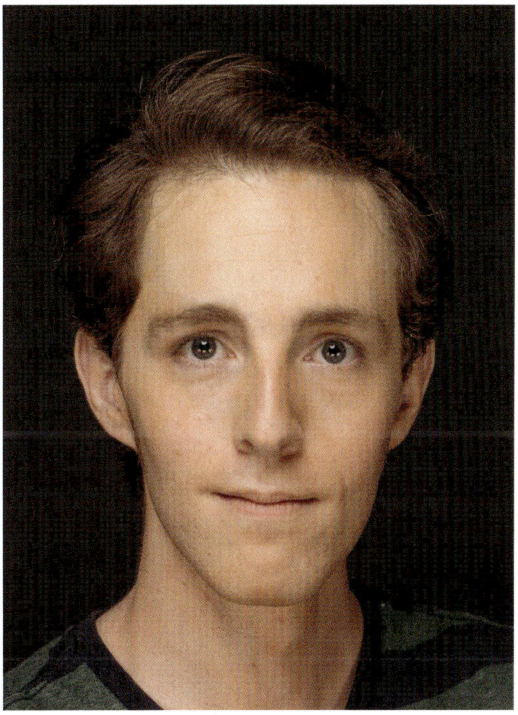

FIGURE 1.1 Step 1

> **Professional Tip:** *You want to be very careful about keeping your makeup sanitary, especially if you're working on someone else. Scoop a little at a time onto a plate or artist's palette with a small spatula. You can re-dip into this makeup without getting germs into the main container. I talk a lot more about safety and sanitation in Appendix 1.*

STEP 1

Apply a layer of cream makeup a shade or two darker than your skin tone to your face, ears and neck. This first layer of makeup is called a **foundation**, also known as **base**. Using a color darker than your skin will make it look like you live outside in the sun. Keep the application a little uneven to give yourself a blotchy skin tone.

There are a lot of ways that you can apply the makeup. Professionals often use makeup brushes and sponges to spread the makeup out over an actor's face. Another option is to just use your fingers. This isn't the most hygienic choice if you're doing the makeup on someone else, but it's fine on your own face.

STEP 2

Pucker your lips as if you are getting ready to give someone a kiss. While your lips are puckered, pat (don't wipe) foundation onto them. When you release your lips, they will have a dry, cracked appearance.

This repeated patting–tapping method of applying makeup is called **stippling**. In the case of the chapped lips, stippling prevents you from filling the cracks with makeup the way brushing or sponging would do. As you'll see in a few steps, it's also a great way to create textures.

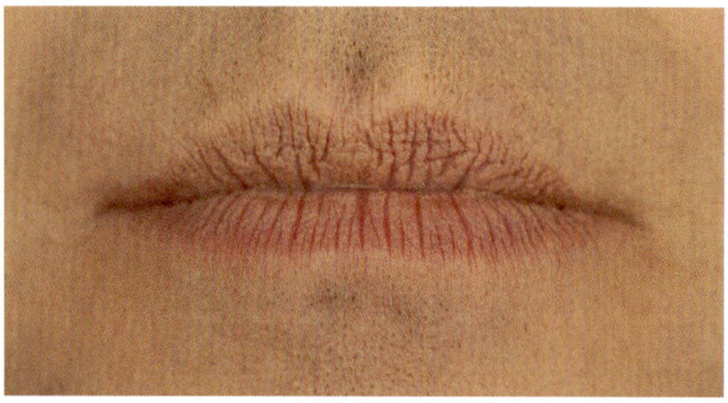

FIGURE 1.2 Step 2

STEP 3

Add a little sunburn-red color to your face, applying it unevenly like the foundation. This will make it look even more like you spend all day outside in the sun. Keep this coat thin: you just want a hint of sunburn, not pizza face.

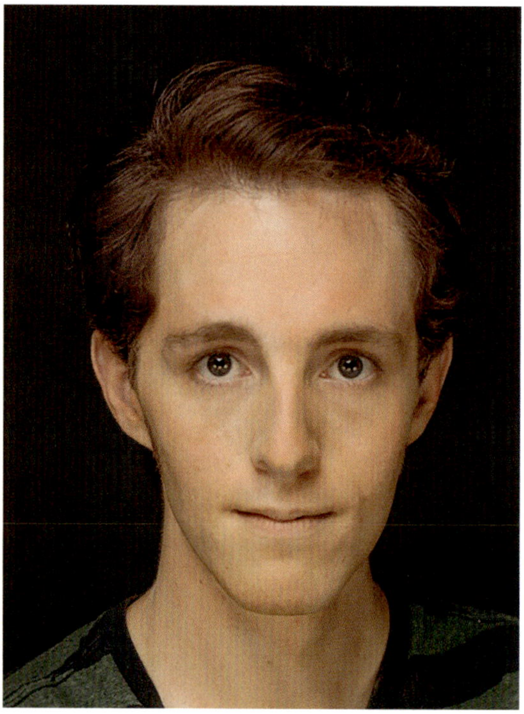

FIGURE 1.3 Step 3

Make the sunburn color most intense on the areas of your face that get the most sun: your forehead, nose, cheekbones and the tops of your ears.

STEP 4

Now that the foundation and sunburn color are in place, you want to **powder** the makeup. If you were to touch your face right now, you would end up with makeup smeared onto your fingers.

Shake some translucent powder (also called "no-color" powder) onto a powder puff. Rub the powder into the puff, then press the puff firmly against your face to **set** the makeup. If there's any

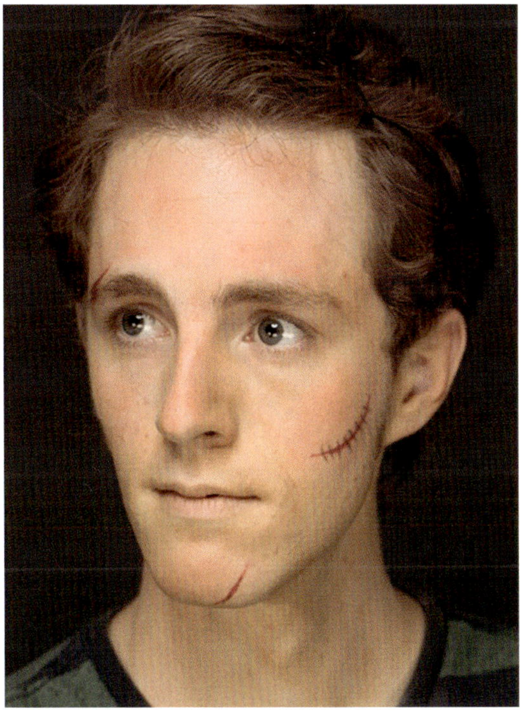

FIGURE 1.4 Step 5

excess powder left on your skin, you can brush it away with a fluffy powder brush.

STEP 5

Use a blood-red makeup pencil to draw a few cuts and scars on your face. To make them look deeper, use a black makeup pencil to darken the middle part of each cut. For stitches, use the black makeup pencil to draw lines across the red ones. These stitches should be perpendicular to the cuts.

STEP 6

Dry your teeth with a tissue, then apply an uneven coat of tooth enamel onto them. It's available in a variety of colors, including black, gold, nicotine and rotten green. Use whichever colors

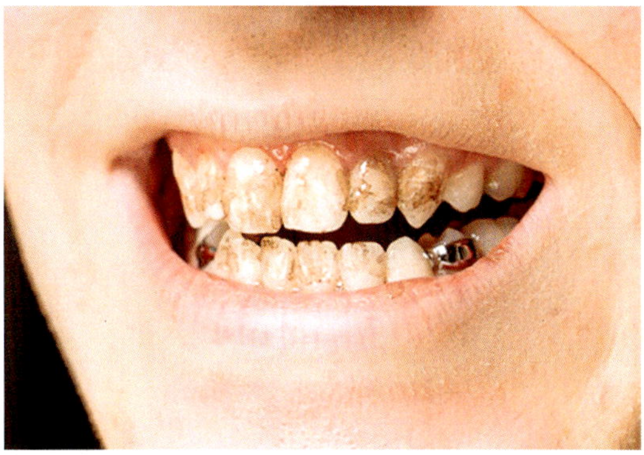

FIGURE 1.5 Step 6

you want to make your teeth look nasty (nicotine is a good start for a pirate). Tooth enamel wears off after a few hours, or you can brush your teeth to remove it at any time.

STEP 7

Cut a piece of black **stipple sponge** into a rounded shape to help prevent any straight lines or repeating patterns in the makeup you're about to apply. If you don't have a stipple sponge, try using a piece of coarse fish tank filter.

Dip the rounded sponge into some black makeup, then gently stipple against your skin to create beard stubble. Add more black makeup to the sponge whenever it starts to run out.

Professional Tip: *After you load the stipple sponge with makeup, tap it a few times against a paper towel before you work on your face. This will remove excess makeup from the sponge so that you don't get big blobs on your skin, which can be really hard to remove without having to start over.*

Add beard stubble onto your face where a real beard would grow. Look at photos of actual stubble if you need inspiration.

If you want it to look more like a beard instead of ungroomed stubble, leave your neck clean and just concentrate on your face and jawline.

STEP 8

This next step is optional: you can carefully powder the beard stubble to help keep it from smearing. You need a light hand, though. It's pretty easy to smear the stippled-on makeup if you're too aggressive with the powder puff. If you don't want to take the risk, you can leave the stubble unpowdered, but be careful not to touch it.

STEP 9

Wear this makeup with a pirate wig and costume. Darken your eyebrows with the black makeup pencil if they're a lot lighter than the wig, as was the case with Jake.

An option that's been very popular for movie pirates lately is black eyeliner. Apply it along your eyelids with a black makeup pencil, then use a cotton swab or makeup brush to smudge it a bit. I chose not to use eyeliner for this makeup, but I added some digitally to show you what it can look like.

You can make this more realistic with advanced scars and cuts (which are covered in the **Wounds and Injuries** chapter) and with real chopped hair stubble (covered in **Laying Hair and Stubble**).

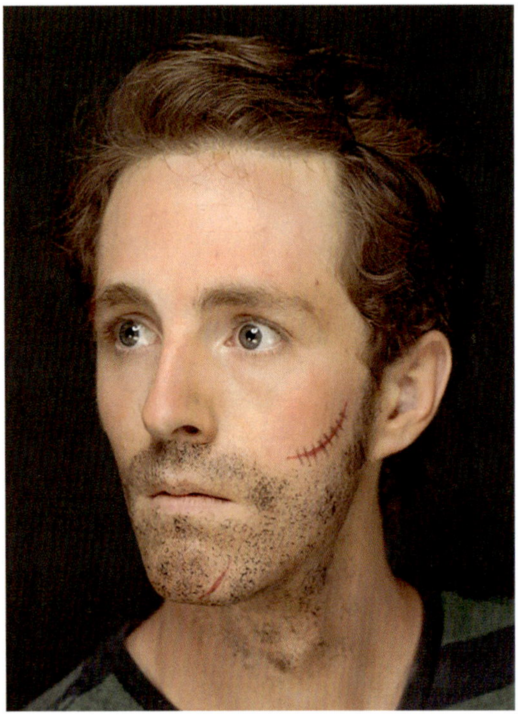

FIGURE 1.6 Step 7

FIGURE 1.7 Never underestimate the power of guyliner

Take some pictures of this makeup, and of every makeup you learn from this book. It's a great way to chart your progress when you're all the way at the end, and of course you're going to want to show off your work to the world!

By the way, if you're going to be doing a lot of makeup on yourself (or on someone else), being sanitary and taking care of your skin is really important. I have some information about that in **Appendix I** if you want to skip ahead and give it a read.

CHAPTER 2

HIGHLIGHT AND SHADOW

One of the most important concepts for a makeup artist to understand is **highlight** and **shadow**. This technique is how an artist makes a flat painting or drawing look three-dimensional. You can also use these powerful tools to completely change the shape of your face using only color.

Highlighting means to make parts of your face lighter so it appears to stand out, while shadowing (also called **contouring**) means you're making things darker to appear more sunken. When you shadow under your cheekbones, for example, it starts to make your face look gaunt and cadaverous. Adding a highlight to the cheekbone itself can intensify the effect.

Figures 2.1–2.3 show the procedure for creating a deep cheek shadow. You can play with the intensity of your shadows and highlights in certain areas to create a more natural effect. When shadowing under your cheeks, for example, shadowing the area right beneath the cheekbone more heavily creates a 3D effect that a single level of shadow doesn't.

Feeling the bone structure under your face can help you to understand the placement of highlight and shadow. Looking at pictures of gaunt faces is also a useful aid. As in any makeup, research beforehand is super helpful.

The easiest way to create custom highlight or shadow is to mix bright or dark colors into

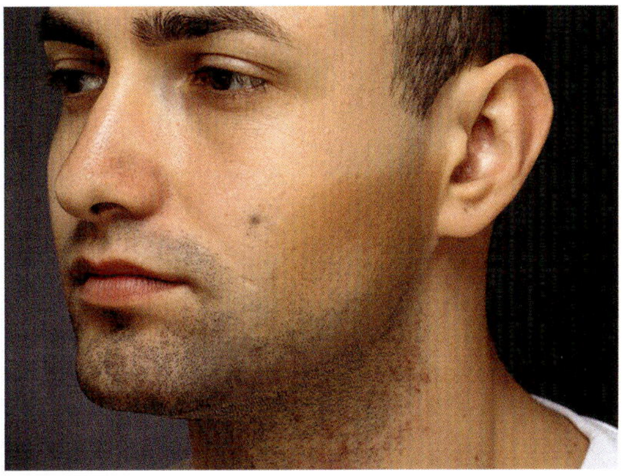

FIGURE 2.1 Basic shadow applied under the cheekbone

FIGURE 2.2 Darker color added to deepen parts of the shadow

your foundation color. Character makeups like the **Vampire** or **Witch** (covered later in this book) will use special colors, but most makeups with normal skin tones use browns to create shadow (black if your skin is very dark) and a very pale beige to create highlight (pale yellow for dark skin). The amount that you mix into your foundation determines how strong the highlight and shadow colors will be.

As you do the makeups in this book, try varying the strengths of your highlights and shadows. The same makeup can be done with several levels of intensity. For example, the **Vampire** makeup coming up can be done with subtle shading to look realistic close up, or with much stronger shadows to read from across the street (or on stage).

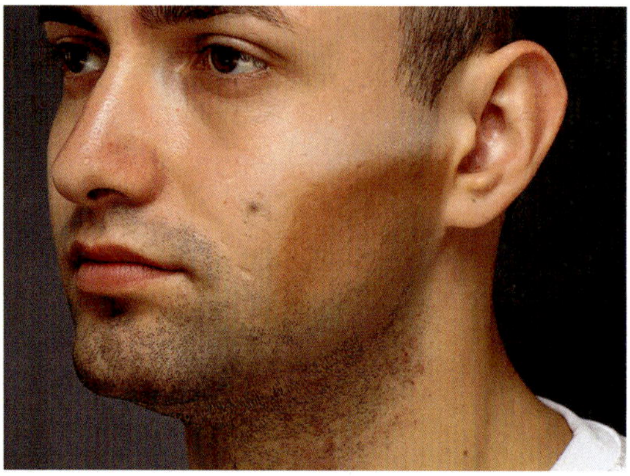

FIGURE 2.3 Highlight on the cheekbone to make it stand out

CHAPTER 3
VAMPIRE

For the **Vampire** makeup, we're going to do the classic look made famous by movies such as *Dracula*. You will only need a few colors to start, but you can dress up the makeup with fangs and blood for a more gruesome effect. This makeup will introduce you to a few more basic concepts that you will use for most of the characters in this book.

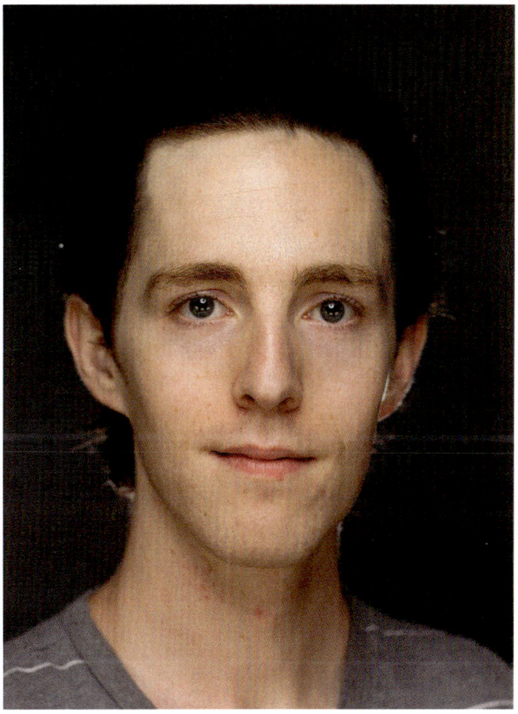

FIGURE 3.1 Step 1

STEP 1

Begin by slicking your hair back. In classic horror movies vampires always have their hair combed back, exposing the entire forehead. Use plenty of hair gel to keep it in place.

If you have light hair and want to darken it, use spray-in black hair color from your local costume shop. Holding a tissue against your hairline can help keep the spray off your skin. It can be washed off with a cotton ball soaked with rubbing alcohol, but it's easier not to make a mess in the first place.

STEP 2

Apply a very pale (not white) foundation to your entire face, neck and ears. As you're changing your face's color so dramatically, you want to cover any exposed skin. Spread the makeup evenly over your skin, being careful not to leave any streaks or lines.

FIGURE 3.2 Step 2

STEP 3

Mix a little dark gray makeup with some foundation to create a shadow color. Add this shadow to the eye sockets, down the sides of the nose, on your temples and under your cheekbones. As you just read in the Highlight and Shadow chapter, the goal is to make your face look sunken, as if you had just crawled out of the grave.

It's important to start with just a little makeup at first. You can always add more if you want your shadows to look darker, but it's a lot harder to take it back off if you apply too much.

Soften the edges of the shadow with a clean brush, sponge or your fingers until it looks like natural contours instead of painted-on lines.

Author's Note: *Some makeup artists like to powder in between each stage of the makeup so they can work on a dryer surface; others like to wait until the end to powder so the different cream colors blend together more easily. Try both and do whichever works best for you.*

STEP 4

Powder the makeup with translucent powder and a powder puff. As before, dust away any excess with a fluffy powder brush.

FIGURE 3.3 Step 3

FIGURE 3.4 Step 5

STEP 5

With a black makeup pencil, thicken your eyebrows to make them look extra sinister. Simulate individual hairs by drawing short strokes, following the direction that the eyebrows grow. This gives you much more realistic eyebrows than you can get by filling them in solid.

Use this same technique to give yourself a widow's peak, extending your hairline down in a point in the middle of your forehead.

STEP 6

Finish your vampire by adding some fangs and a trickle of blood dribbling down from your mouth.

You can learn how to make fangs in the **Fangs and Claws** chapter, and blood in the **Blood** chapter.

CHAPTER 4
GHOST

The **Ghost** makeup is similar to the **Vampire** . . . at least at first. You will incorporate the same basic steps as for the Vampire, but with some different colors and details. It's a good example of how a few minor changes can result in a very different character. This tortured soul might be found lurking in an old graveyard, luring unsuspecting victims to their doom.

STEP 1

Use a black makeup pencil to draw veins on your forehead and neck, starting at your hairline and collar and sketching them toward the center of your face. Look at pictures of lightning bolts as examples of random vein shapes. Purple or maroon also make good, creepy vein colors.

Professional Tip: *Makeup artists often use reference photos when creating a character. These photos can come from books, magazines or the internet. Nature is full of amazing colors, patterns and designs that you can incorporate into your makeup.*

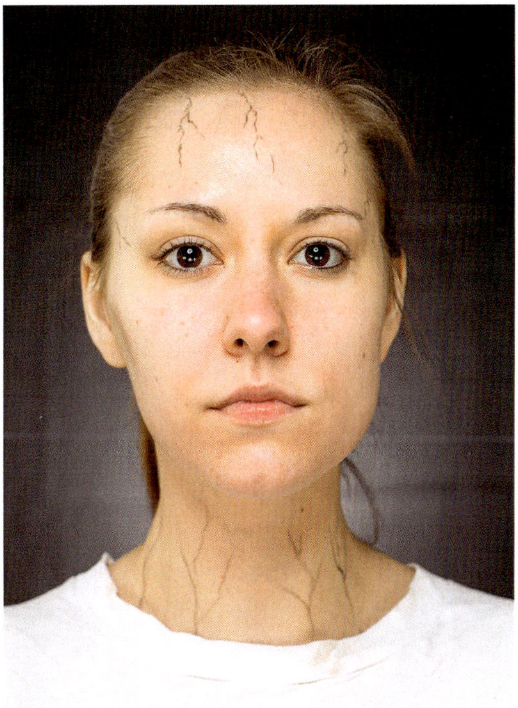

FIGURE 4.1 Step 1

STEP 2

Apply white foundation to your face, neck and ears using a stippling motion similar to the **Pirate**'s foundation, but instead of a light coat fully cover your face with an uneven, mottled white.

FIGURE 4.2 Lightning bolt

Credit: Shutterstock

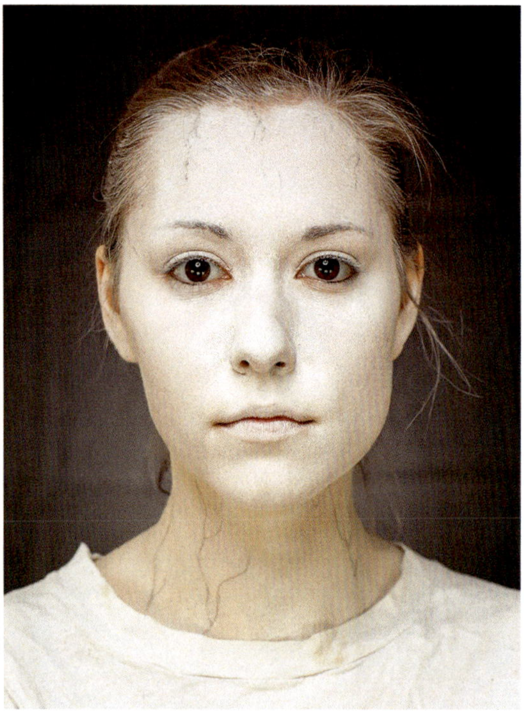

FIGURE 4.3 Step 2

The veins will still show slightly beneath the foundation. Make them darker with the makeup pencil if you need to, but keep them subtle. They should appear to be under your skin, not drawn on top.

STEP 3

Mix a shadow color using purple and gray makeup. Use it to shadow your eye sockets, your temples and under your cheekbones, as well as the dip under your nose and the deep area between your lower lip and chin.

You also want to shadow your **nasolabial folds** (the smile lines that go from your nose down to your mouth). Draw a line along the natural crease, then blend the shadow upward from that line onto your cheek. Be sure to hook this shadow up on top of your nostrils; don't just stop at the corner of your nose.

This particular shadow is an example of a **hard edge** and **soft edges**. Keep these terms in your brain: I'll talk about them in more detail on the next makeup.

STEP 4

Use the purple-gray makeup to draw lines coming down from below your eyes. Keep these lines somewhat faint; you'll fill them in with darker makeup in the next step.

Draw more purple-gray lines extending out from your lips as if they are cracking open.

STEP 5

Use black makeup to deepen the shadows, as shown in the **Highlight and Shadow** chapter. Use the same black to paint thinner lines within the purple-gray ones coming from your eyes and lips and to paint the lips themselves black.

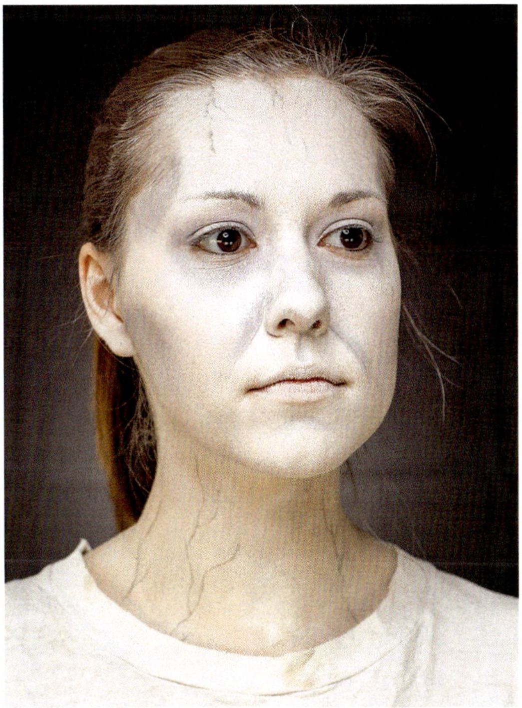

FIGURE 4.4 Step 3

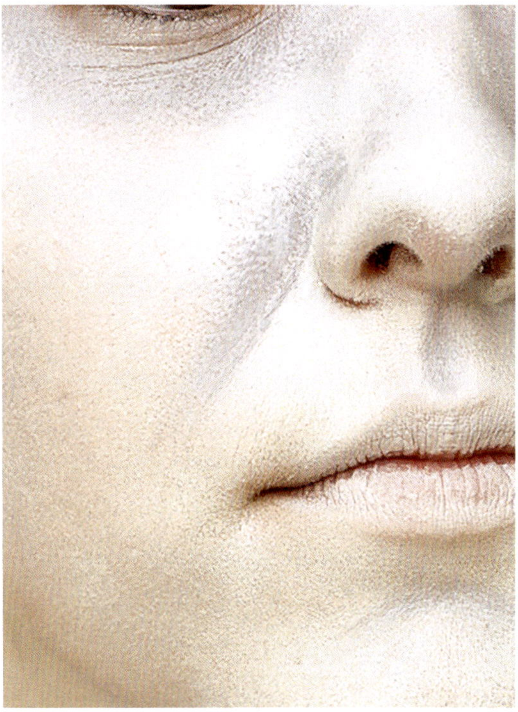

FIGURE 4.5 Step 3 (Detail)

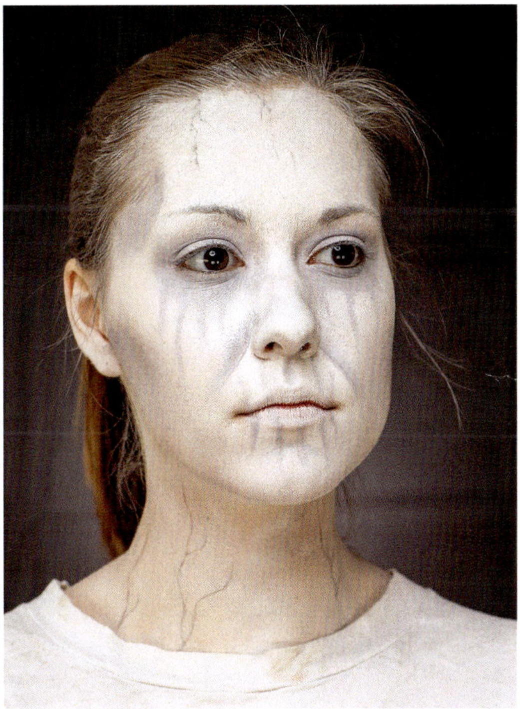

FIGURE 4.6 Step 4

FIGURE 4.7 Step 5

STEP 6

Powder the entire makeup if you haven't already.

STEP 7

Squeeze a little hair gel into a spray bottle, then fill it with water and shake it until the two are mixed. Spray this gel–water mixture onto your hair to wet it down and let it hang in your face in strings. Your hair will look darker when it's wet, but if it's *really* fair you can use a dark spray-in color or rub in some dark makeup powder after you spray it. The gel will keep your hair looking stringy even after it has dried.

Put on the shabbiest clothes that you own, ideally something from a thrift store that you can really mess up. You can also use items such as gauze, strips of cloth or even fake cobwebs from a Halloween store to accent the costume.

This makeup is a good one to try a few times playing with different colors. Try adding some more purple to the shadow for a less black and white effect. What about green for a radioactive ghost? Maybe dark red instead of black under the eyes so it looks like she's crying tears of blood? The possibilities are endless.

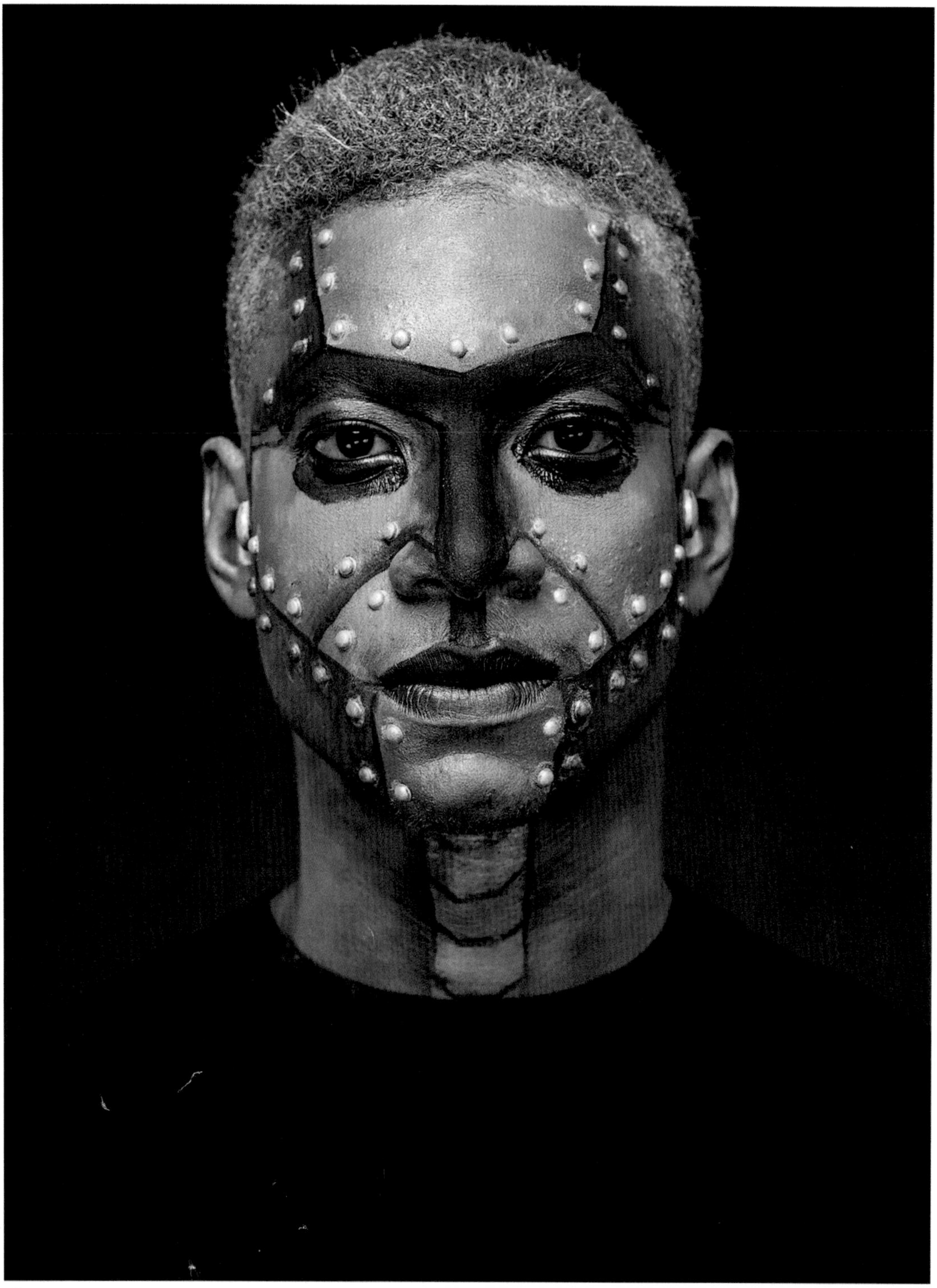

CHAPTER 5
ROBOT

Robots appear in all varieties of science fiction stories, and more and more they're beginning to appear in real life. A human-shaped robot is called an *android*, and it's a fun makeup to create because you will turn your rounded face into flat surfaces and hard angles.

Take a look at the shapes in Figure 5.1. One of them has a round surface, and the other has flat sides and sharp corners. It's easy to tell which is square and which is round by looking at their tops, but what if you just looked at the middle portion, in Figure 5.2?

You can still tell because the highlight and shadow on the left have a **hard edge**, whereas the highlight and shadow on the right have a **soft edge** – it fades smoothly from dark to light and back again. Usually in makeup we deal with soft edges (like the shadow under your cheekbone fading away to nothing), but the Robot is going to use hard edges to turn your face into a series of flat surfaces that join together at sharp angles.

Before doing the makeup, I took a photo of Dan and did a quick concept sketch, dividing his face into a series of flat planes. I played with several variations before I settled on the design shown in Figure 5.3 (I'll show you how to do this yourself in the **Character Design** chapter).

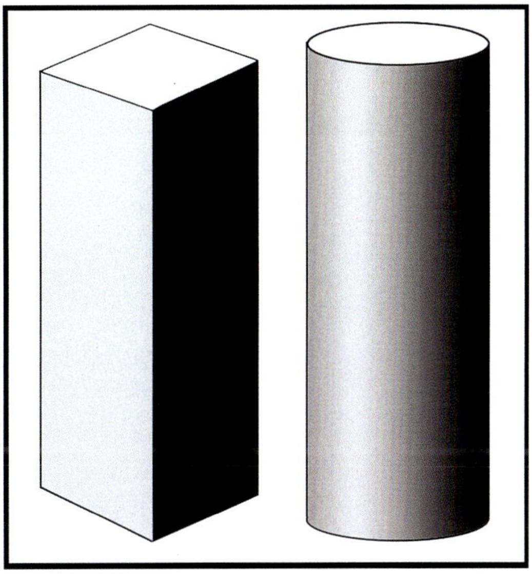

FIGURE 5.1

Credit: Christopher Payne

FIGURE 5.2

Credit: Christopher Payne

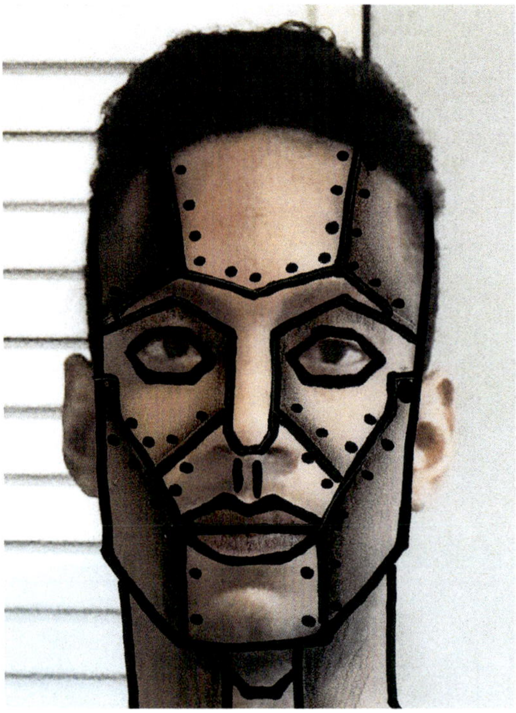

FIGURE 5.3 RoboDan

Credit: Christopher Payne

FIGURE 5.4 Step 1

STEP 1

Spray your hair with silver hair color. If your hair is long, slick it back with hair gel and let it dry. Don't worry about cleaning any silver off your skin: you'll just be covering it with more silver anyway.

Another option is to skip the hair and wear a metallic hat or helmet when the makeup is done.

STEP 2

Draw the dividing lines onto your face with a black makeup pencil. Your lines don't have to be perfect: they'll be mostly covered with makeup anyway. Right now, you're just sketching it out.

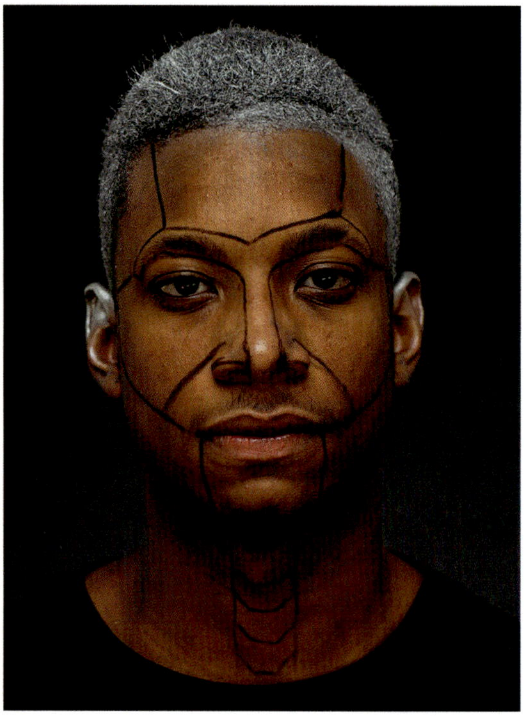

FIGURE 5.5 Step 2

STEP 3

Now we're going to use a material that you probably don't think of in terms of makeup: googly eyes. These are going to be the rivets on the robot's face.

Apply a dot of **spirit gum** where you want the first rivet to go. Spirit gum is a theatrical glue that can be found in any costume shop. It's safe to use on your skin, and can be removed with **spirit gum remover** or rubbing alcohol.

Let the spirit gum get tacky (you can speed this up by tapping it with your finger) and then press a googly eye in place. Apply a thin coat of **liquid latex** on top with a cotton swab. The latex will give a better surface for the makeup to stick. Because the makeup will be a slightly different color on the latex than on your skin, try to get the latex only on the plastic eye.

Never let liquid latex get into your hair or onto your clothes. It will be very hard to remove it later. You may even have to cut it out!

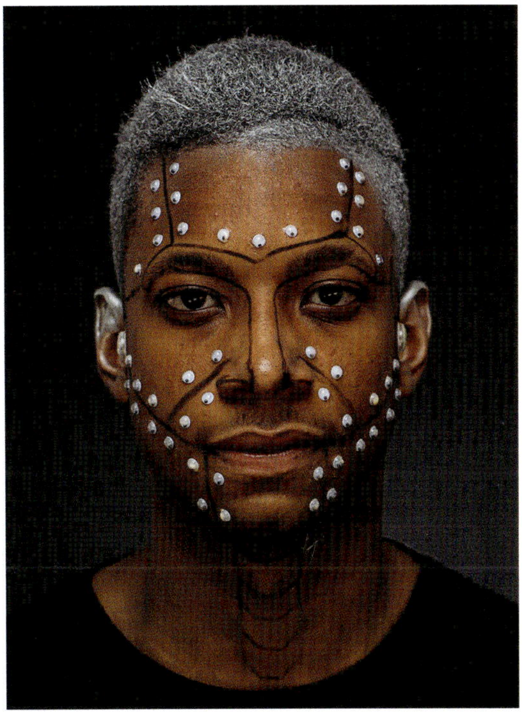

FIGURE 5.6 Step 4

STEP 4

Add more rivets anywhere you want it to look like the different sections of your face have been bolted together like pieces of metal. You can dry the latex faster with a hairdryer.

STEP 5

Apply silver makeup to your entire face with a makeup sponge. Stipple the makeup on with the sponge instead of brushing it to make sure the rivets don't get pulled off (glue them back on if you need to).

Once this is done, draw the lines back onto your face with black makeup and a fine brush. Now is the time to take extra care that your lines are perfectly straight, which is a lot harder than it sounds. A ruler or other straight edge can help.

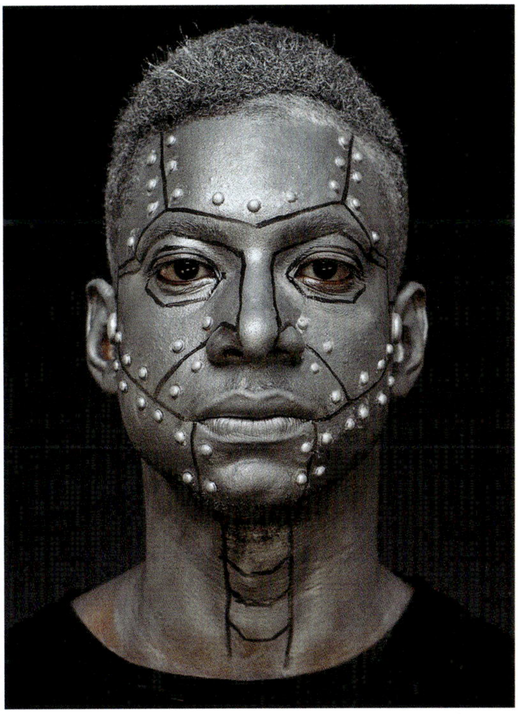

FIGURE 5.7 Step 5

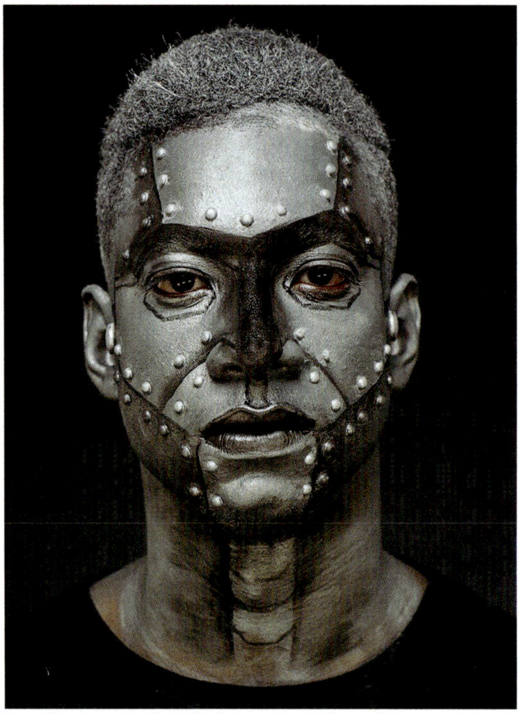

FIGURE 5.8 Step 6

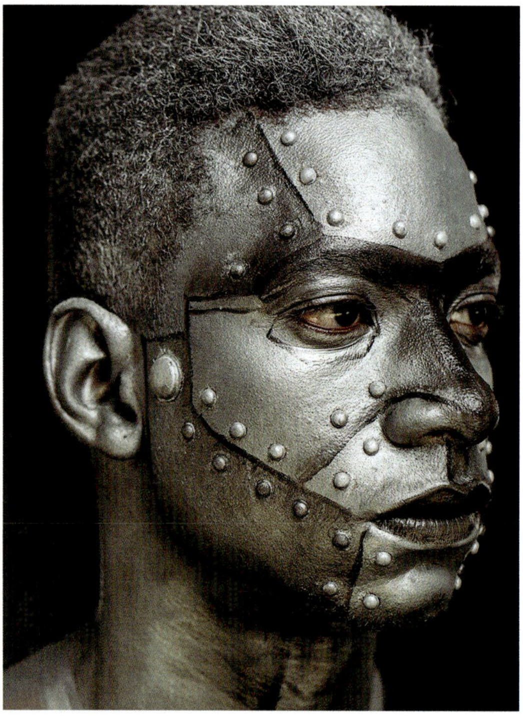

FIGURE 5.9 Step 6 (side view)

STEP 6

Begin adding shadows, starting at the drawn lines and blending away from them to create the illusion of flat plates and sharp angles. For this character, the temples, eye sockets, lips and the sides of the jaw, nose and neck are shadowed. Your shadowing may be different depending on the layout of your lines, but you will typically blend away from the center of your face. I have added some arrows to an image to show what I mean (Figure 5.10).

STEP 7

Powder the makeup once you're done.

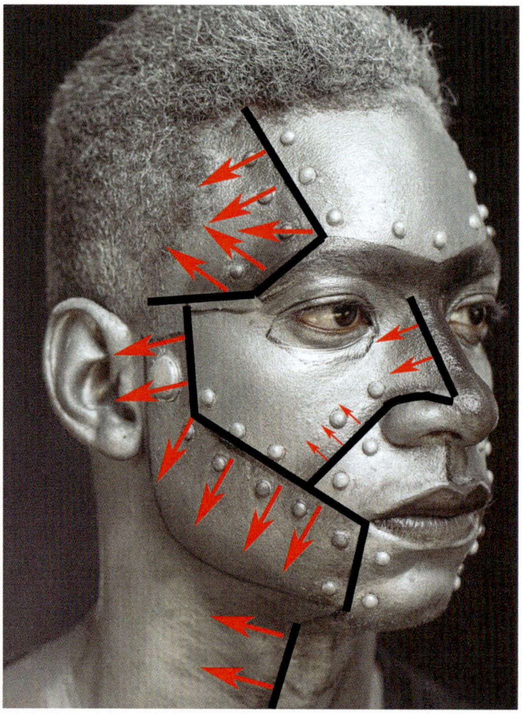

FIGURE 5.10 Step 6 (blending direction detail)

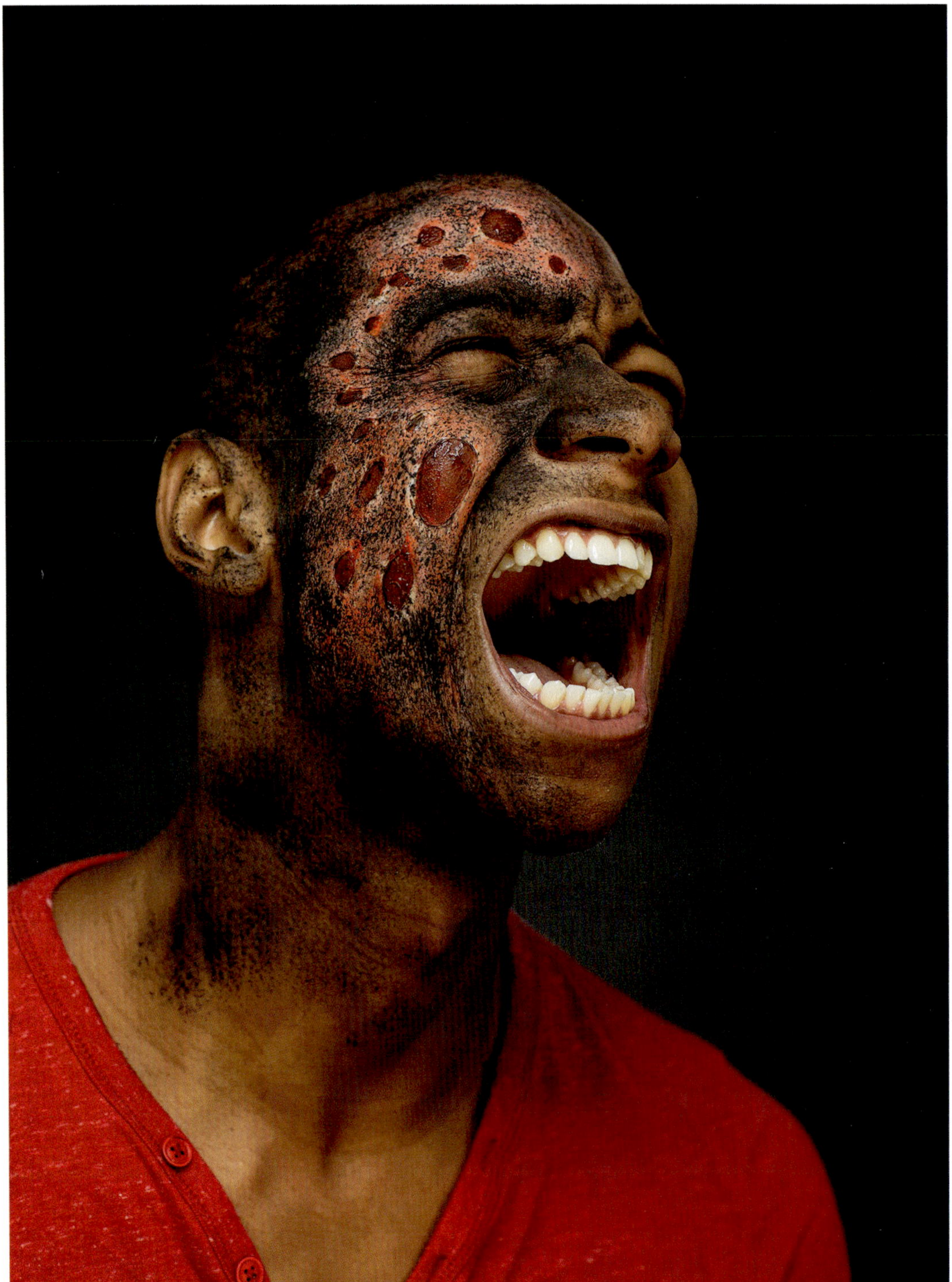

CHAPTER 6
BASIC BURN

Burns are one of the most painful injuries that a person can receive, and a gory burn makeup always gets a great reaction from people. In this makeup, you will use liquid latex to a greater extent than you did with the **Robot** character. Instead of just using it to cover the rivets, now you're going to use latex to create large areas of texture.

STEP 1

Apply a few thin coats of liquid latex to the areas on your face you want burned, drying each one before adding the next. You can apply the latex with a latex-free makeup sponge, or you can use a cheap brush so long as you grease it with dish soap first to protect the bristles.

Once again, be very careful not to get the liquid latex in your hair or on your clothes.

> **Professional Tip:** *Latex likes to stick to itself. Most makeup sponges are made of latex and they may pull any liquid latex you're working with back off your skin. For this makeup I cut sponges out of a 1-inch-thick sheet of craft foam from the local fabric store. They're about the same size and shape, but as they're latex-free there was less danger of sticking.*

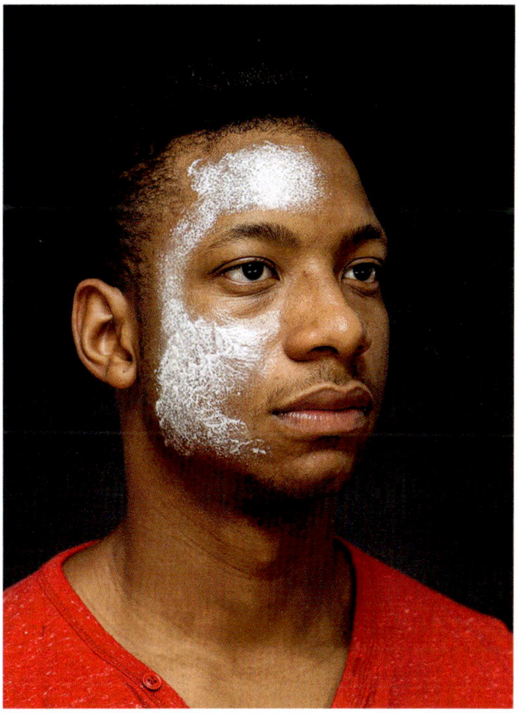

FIGURE 6.1 Step 1

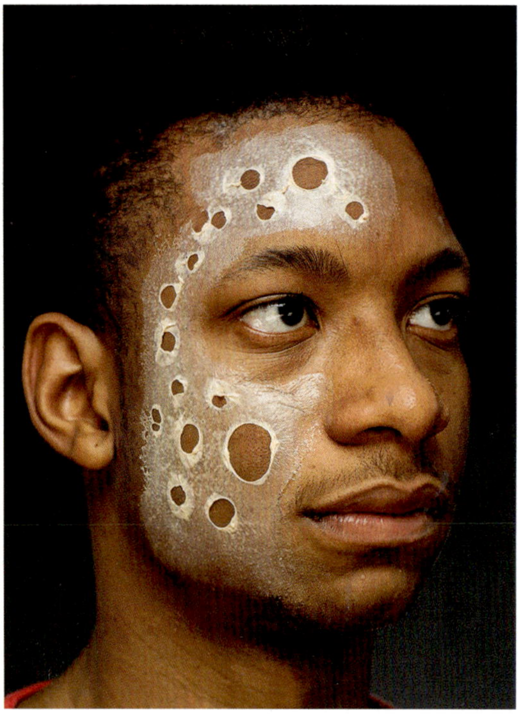

FIGURE 6.2 Step 2

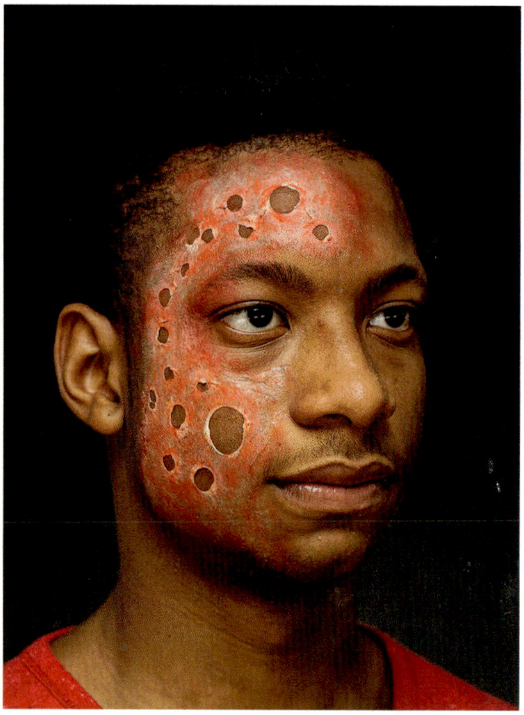

FIGURE 6.3 Step 4

STEP 2

Pick holes in the latex with your fingernails or a pair of tweezers once it's dry. The holes should be different sizes, some large and some small.

An alternative method is to pull a small section of latex away from your skin and then snip it with a pair of cuticle scissors. Be careful not to cut yourself if you go this route!

Roll the latex back on itself from the center of each hole to create a raised ring, which gives the burn a more three-dimensional appearance. This time you're using the fact that unpowdered latex sticks to itself to your advantage.

STEP 3

Once you're happy with your wounds, powder the latex to set it and keep it from sticking any more than it already has.

STEP 4

Stipple a few layers of pink and red makeup onto your face around the open wounds. These colors will make the skin surrounding the wounds look raw and irritated. Keep the color mottled and irregular; if you blend it together too much it can start to look fake.

STEP 5

Stipple black makeup onto your face with a coarse stipple sponge to simulate charred flesh. Try not to get too much inside the wounds as that will just give you more work in the next step.

Extend the charred flesh past the edges of the latex and fade it out into your skin.

STEP 6

Remove any black makeup within the open wounds with cotton swabs dipped in water. You want to restore as much of the natural skin color within the wounds as you can. If the makeup is really stubborn, use liquid makeup remover instead of water.

STEP 7

Fill the wounds with bright red makeup to give the appearance of burned, irritated flesh. Once this is done, apply maroon around the edges of each wound, blending it toward the center, to give the wounds depth.

STEP 8

Smear a bit of baby oil or glycerin into the open wounds. It will make the wounds seem like they're shiny and raw and really set them apart from the dry, charred skin.

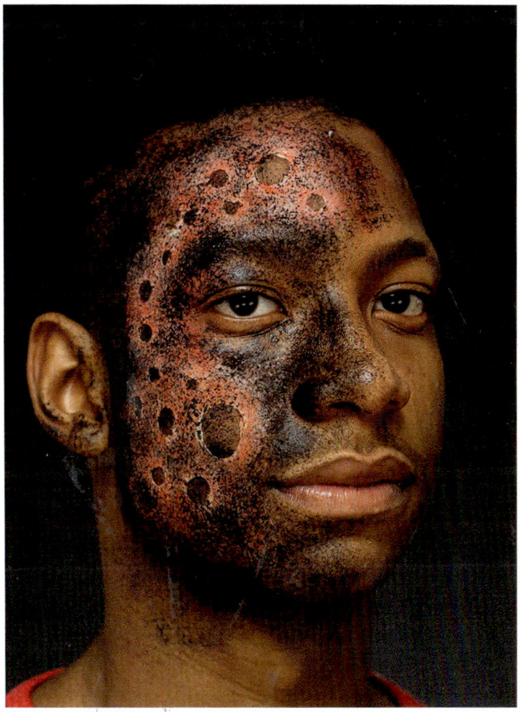

FIGURE 6.4 Step 5

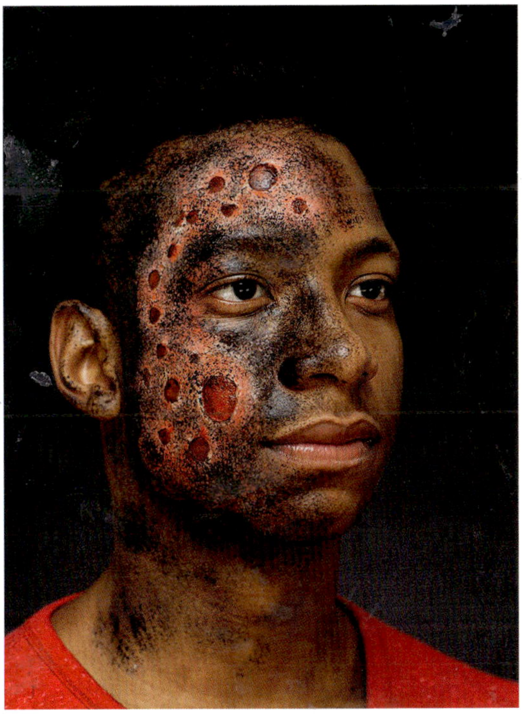

FIGURE 6.5 Step 7

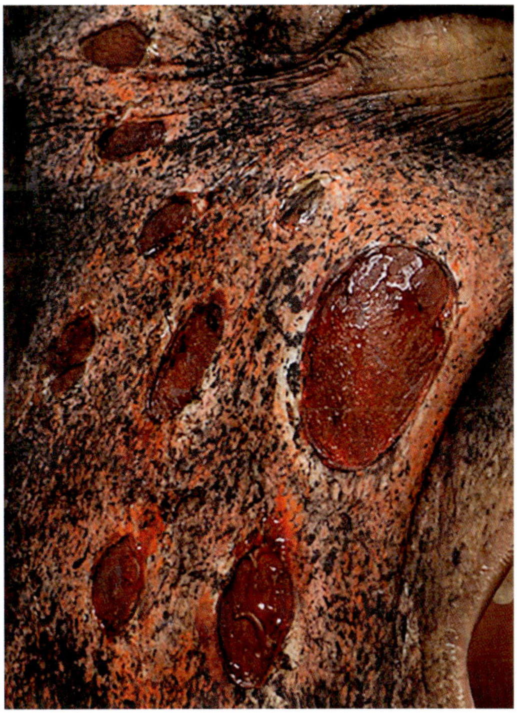

FIGURE 6.6 Step 7 (detail)

Professional Tip: *An alternative to using baby oil to shine up a makeup is to use any personal lubricant gel, such as KY. If you're doing makeup on someone else, you may want to decant it into a different bottle first to avoid an awkward conversation. The squeezy bottle of KY at my makeup station is simply labeled "shiny."*

To remove the latex you can either work a brush with makeup remover under it to tease it away from your skin, or steam it for a few minutes with a hot washcloth before peeling the latex off. Dan had a lot of fun with that part.

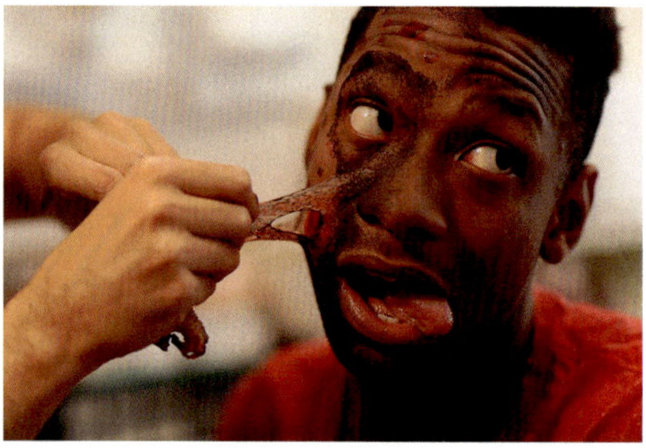

FIGURE 6.7

I can't say I blame him. Just try peeling it off without making silly faces, I dare you. I've never been able to.

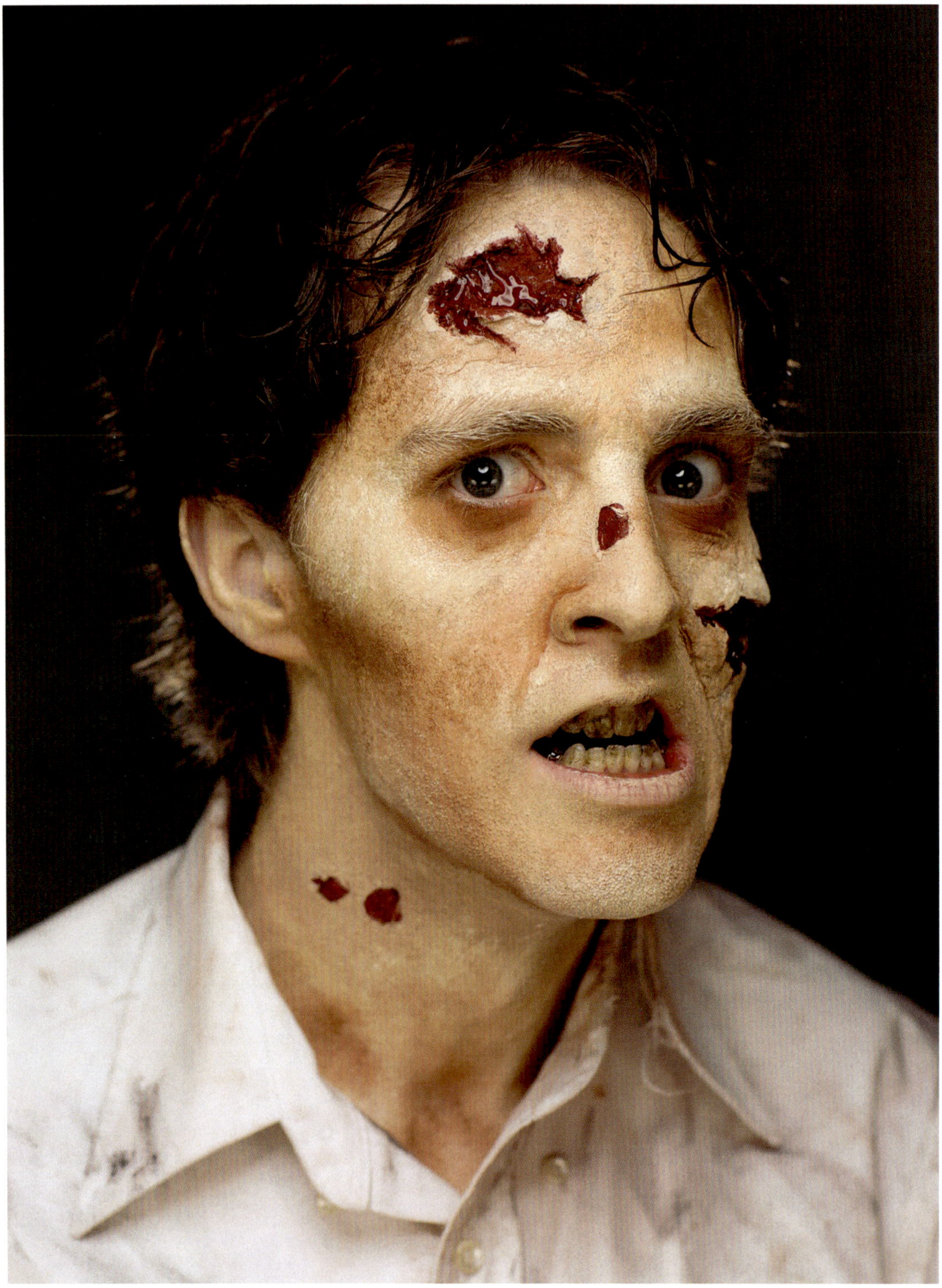

CHAPTER 7

BASIC ZOMBIE

Zombies! They're one of the most popular monsters out there, especially these days. A zombie makeup is a lot of fun because there are so many different ways you can do it. You're only limited by your imagination when it comes to wounds, skin texture and other details.

This character will bring together many techniques from the makeups you have done so far, while introducing a new material: **nose putty**. It'll be a good review before we move on to some more advanced stuff.

STEP 1

Pull a few cotton balls apart into little piles of cotton fluff. You're going to glue this fluff onto your skin to give the nose putty something to grab onto.

STEP 2

Brush some spirit gum onto your face where you want your first zombie wound to go. Let the spirit gum get tacky, then press some of your cotton fluff into it. Once the spirit gum has completely dried, pull off any excess cotton so it doesn't get in your way later.

STEP 3

Pull a pinch of nose putty out of the container and knead it between your fingers until it softens. Softer putty is usually easier to work with than firm, but you need to be more careful not to damage it after it's been applied. Roll the putty into a sausage shape.

Nose putty can be very sticky, but using a little hair gel on your fingertips while you work can help keep it from sticking to your fingers.

STEP 4

Use the putty sausages to outline where you want the wound to go. Smooth the outer edge into your skin, while leaving the inner side raised (this is the edge of your wound). Extend the outer edge of the putty a bit past the cotton fluff,

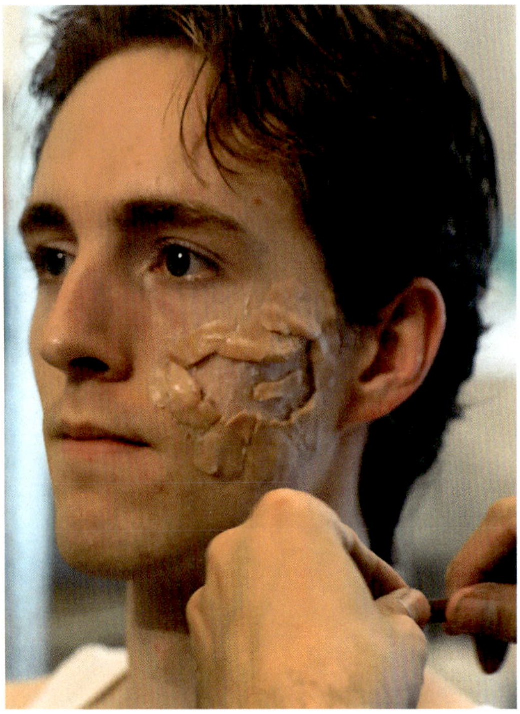

FIGURE 7.1 Step 4 in progress

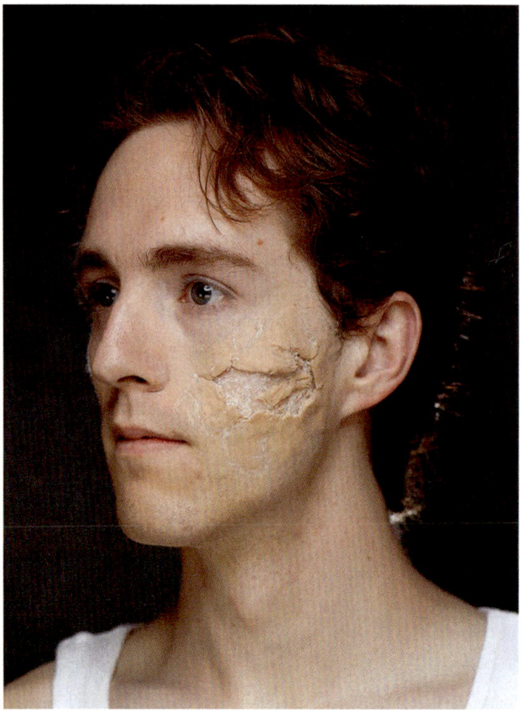

FIGURE 7.2 Step 6

otherwise the edges won't smoothly blend into your skin.

STEP 5

Use a popsicle stick or similar tool to sculpt the putty on your face, creating the finished shape. Zombie wounds should be raw and irregular, like torn flesh.

STEP 6

Stipple a couple of thin coats of liquid latex over the nose putty, extending it a bit past the edges onto your skin. Powder once you're done. The latex will seal the putty, helping it stay stuck to your face. It also gives you a painting surface that's less likely to get damaged when you touch it.

STEP 7

Add more wounds wherever you want them. The nose putty holds best to bony areas on your face that don't move much, like the forehead, cheekbones, nose and chin. Avoid areas with lots of movement like your neck; the putty will work itself loose from those areas pretty quickly. Seal each wound with liquid latex.

STEP 8

Add some picked-open wounds on additional areas of your face and neck, the same way you did with the **Basic Burn** makeup.

STEP 9

Mix a few drops of castor oil into a pale cream foundation to create **rubber mask**

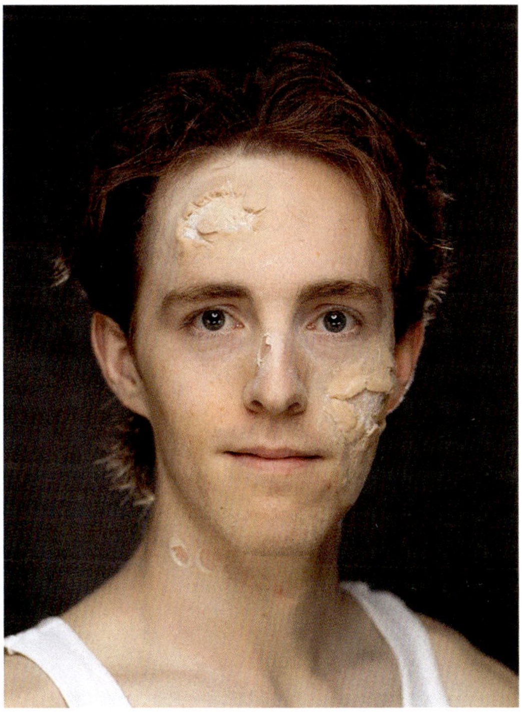

FIGURE 7.3 Step 8

FIGURE 7.4 Makeup sponge with torn edges

Credit: Christopher Payne

greasepaint (RMG), which is a special kind of makeup that is used on latex. Ordinary cream makeup discolors on latex as the oils are absorbed into the rubber, but RMG will keep its color.

STEP 10

Tear the end off of a makeup sponge to create an irregular texture. Use the torn sponge to stipple the RMG over your exposed skin in a mottled pattern. Then, stipple a darker layer of foundation on top of the first layer, again keeping things mottled and uneven. This layering of different skin tones will start to create a broken-up effect.

You can use natural sea sponges to get the same effect if you don't feel like tearing up makeup sponges.

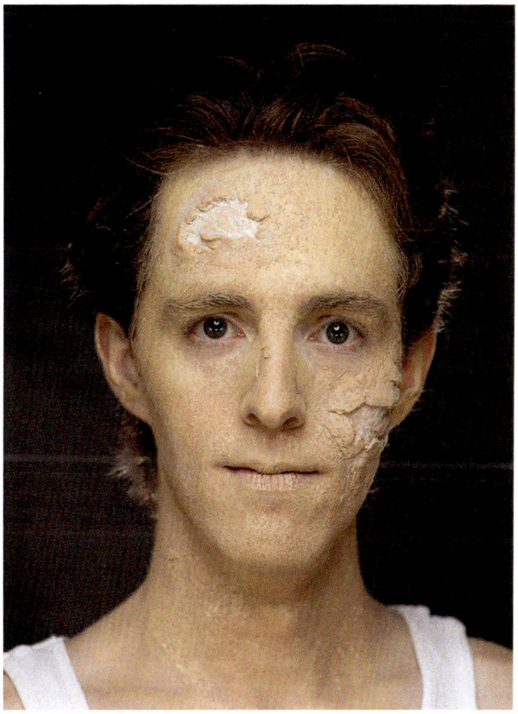

FIGURE 7.5 Step 10

STEP 11

Apply shadows to the hollows of your face, similar to the ones you did for the **Ghost** makeup. In addition, shadow underneath your jawline and along the cords on your neck. Reference photos of people with emaciated faces can help you figure out where to place your highlights and shadows to help your skin look sunken in.

Stipple this shadow with a fresh torn sponge rather than brushing it to make your skin look even more uneven.

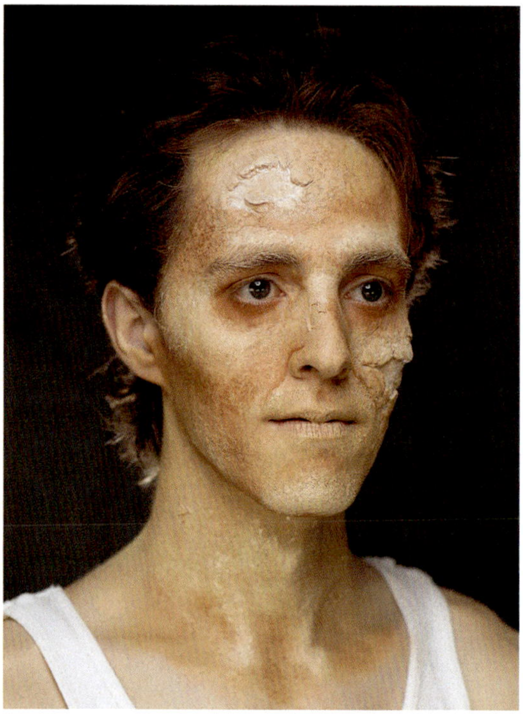

FIGURE 7.6 Step 12

STEP 12

Apply a highlight color around your eye sockets, on your cheekbones and on your chin to pop out your bone structure.

STEP 13

Fill the wounds with either a blood-red color for a fresh zombie or a brownish red for an old, dry zombie. If the wounds are looking flat, add a little highlight along the edges to accentuate them.

STEP 14

Finish with tooth enamel and stage blood. Mess up your hair and put on some old, ratty clothes to complete the character.

To remove the putty, scrape a piece of thread against your skin to slice the putty off. Then, use adhesive remover to take off the glue and leftover cotton.

Figure 7.7 is a picture of me removing a wound on Jake's chin that I ended up not wanting to use. That's the beauty of makeup: if there's something you don't like, just take it off!

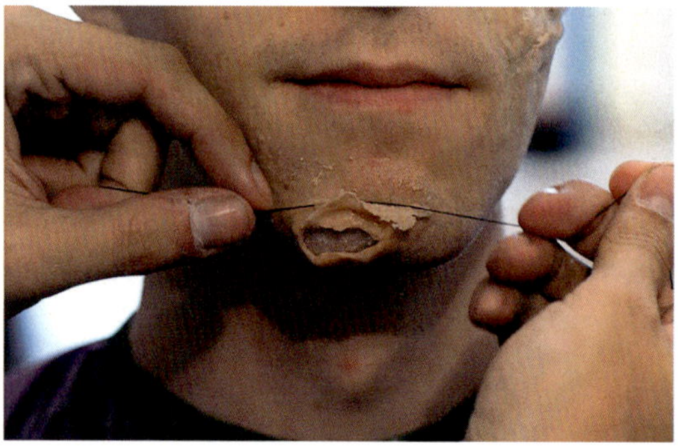

FIGURE 7.7

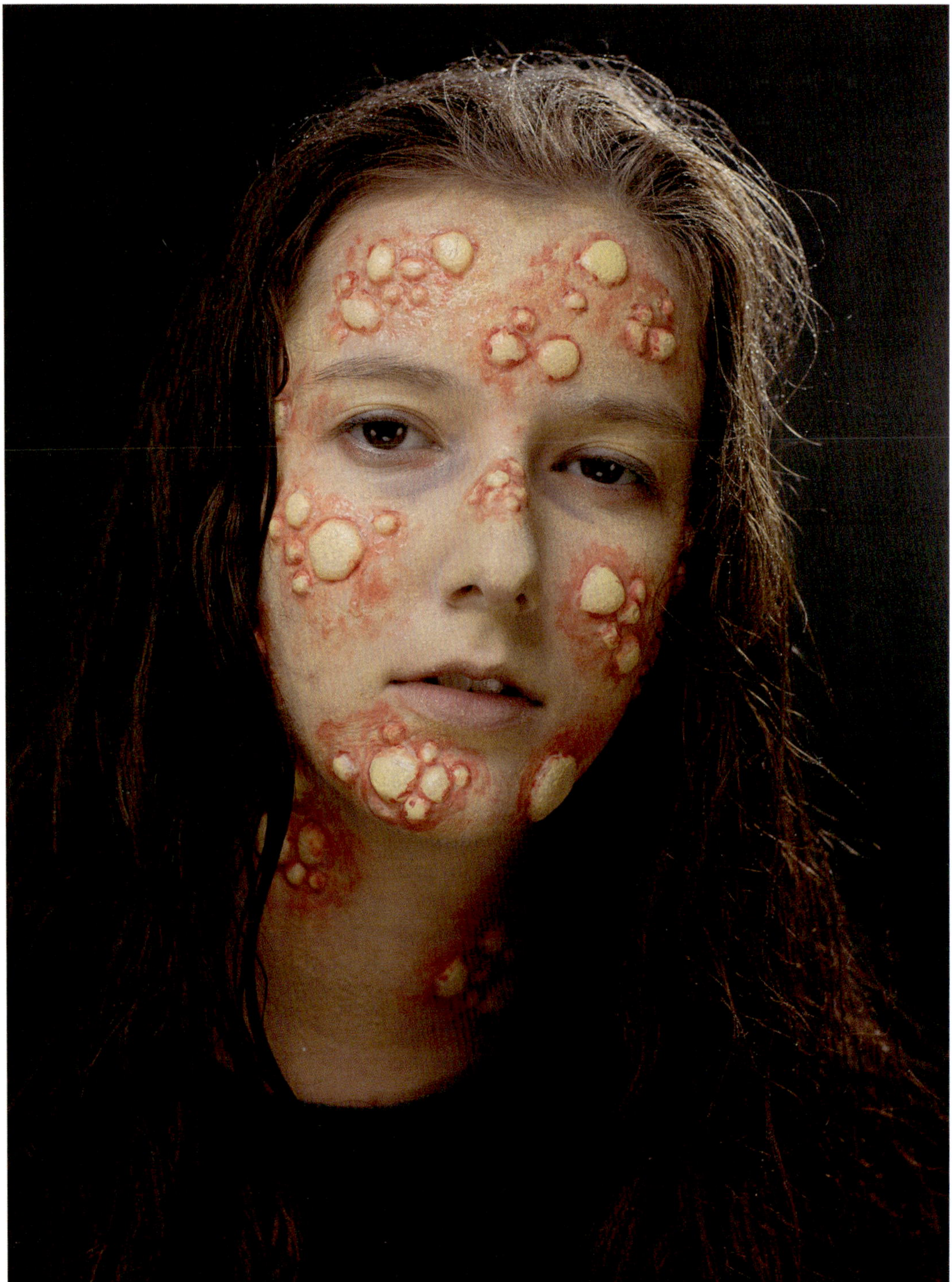

CHAPTER 8
PLAGUE

The **Plague** is a generic term used to describe several diseases that have ravaged humanity throughout history. A disease makeup such as this is a fun way to gross out your friends and family, as no one likes being around sick people. You can be as subtle or as extreme as you want with your plague, depending on how disgusting you want to be.

STEP 1

You're going to begin by creating boils all over your face and neck. Originally, I did a version of this makeup using more googly eyes for the boils, but they ended up looking a little too uniform and not very organic. For nice random boils, I used unflavored gelatin to make them in advance. There are several brands available at grocery stores, though Knox is the brand most makeup artists are familiar with. Knox gelatin is sold in handy little packets, making it easy to mix up small amounts.

Mix one tablespoon of gelatin powder, one tablespoon of boiling water and a quarter-teaspoon of glycerin in a small container. Stir this mixture quickly with a craft stick or butter knife and then let drops fall onto a sheet of wax paper. These drops make great boils when they cool and they're already a nasty yellowish color.

The boils should be used fairly soon after you make them; they will dry out and get hard before too long. The glycerin helps to slow the drying-out process, but they won't last forever. Store them in the fridge if they need to last a couple of days.

Professional Tip: *You want to work quickly while the hot gelatin is runny to get the best drips. As it cools, it will thicken and get stringy, which doesn't work for this makeup. We'll use stringy gelatin later in the book!*

STEP 2

Use spirit gum to apply the boils to your skin in clusters, with a few single ones here and there. You can experiment with grouping different sizes and even gluing a second layer on top of the first.

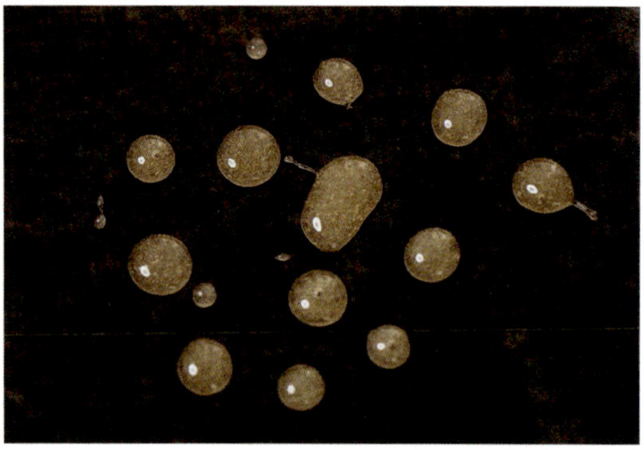

FIGURE 8.1 Gelatin Boils

Credit: Christopher Payne

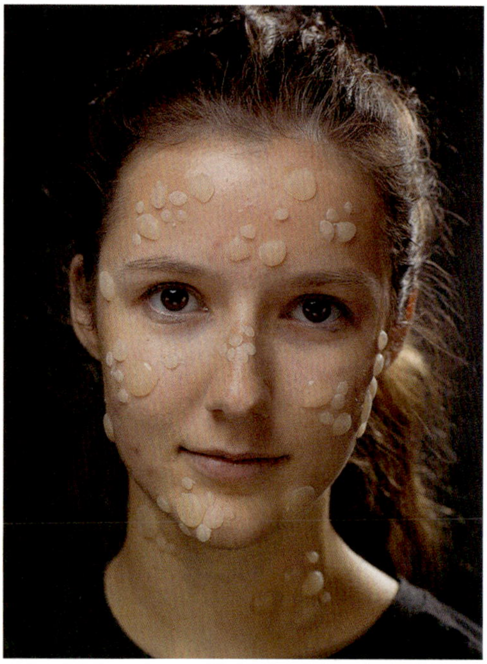

FIGURE 8.2 Step 2

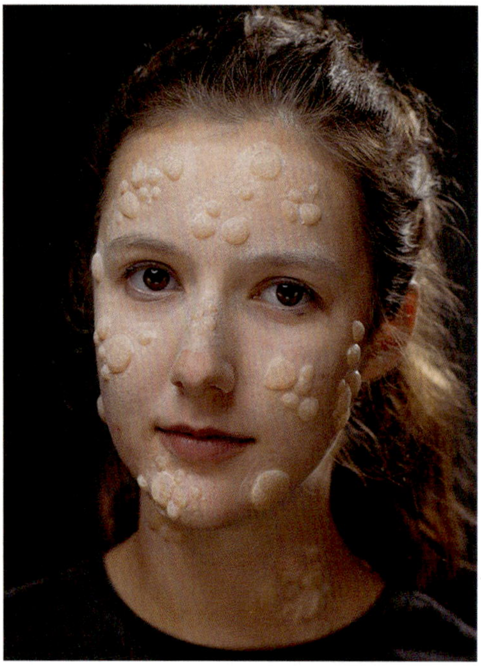

FIGURE 8.3 Step 3

STEP 3

Stipple a few layers of liquid latex over the boils to create a film over them, making them look like they're under your skin. This is the same as the **Robot** rivets, except this time you want to extend the latex onto your skin.

You can also pick open sores in the latex on your skin to make it look like some of the boils have popped (like you did for the **Basic Burn**). Powder the latex once everything is in place.

STEP 4

Stipple a pale yellowish foundation color to your face and neck to help you look sick. It should be irregular: the last thing you want is nice smooth skin for this makeup. Apply the yellow more heavily on top of the boils to make them stand out.

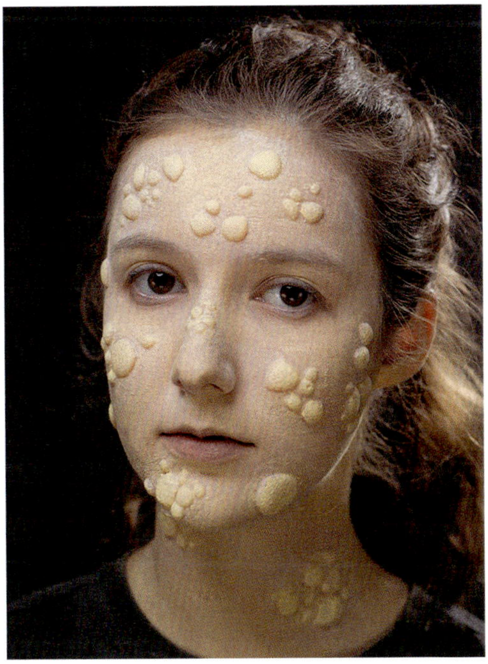

FIGURE 8.4 Step 4

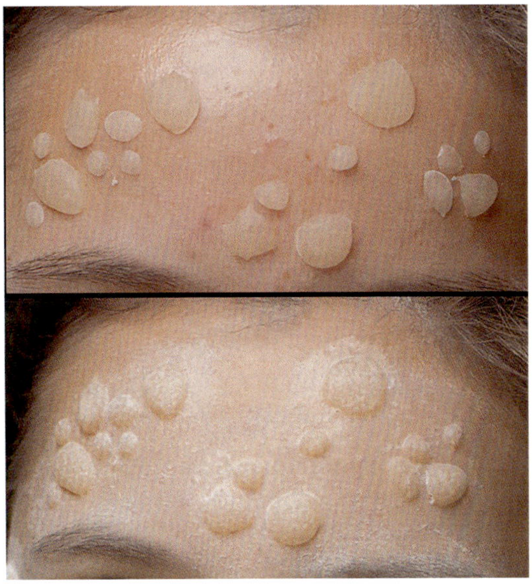

FIGURE 8.5 Boils before and after latex

STEP 5

Apply a faint reddish-pink color around each of the boils to make your skin look irritated. It should fade naturally into your skin, without a hard edge. You can get a more mottled application by stippling the makeup on with a brush instead of painting it on.

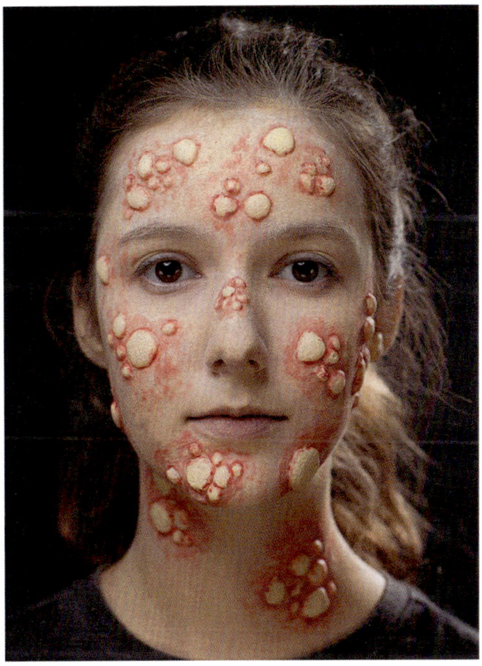

FIGURE 8.6 Steps 5 and 6

STEP 6

Once the pinkish color is in place, go back and use a brush to stipple a small amount of darker red makeup around each boil. You just want a tiny bit to accentuate them and make them look infected. Use the same red to fill in any open sores.

STEP 7

Darken the circles under your eyes with a purple-gray to make yourself look more sickly and give

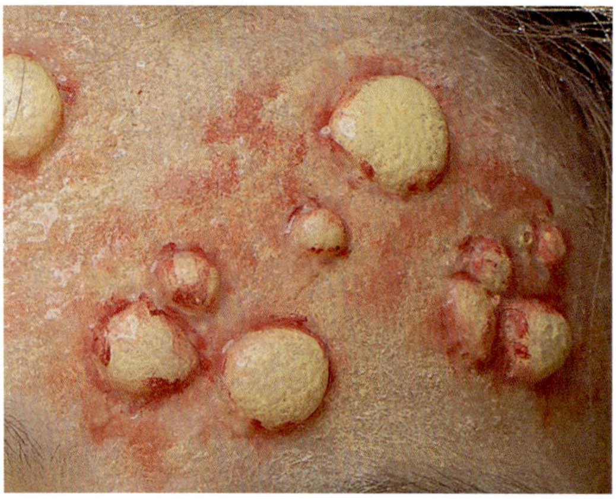

FIGURE 8.7 Steps 5 and 6 (detail)

yourself cracked lips using the foundation the same way you did for the **Pirate**. For a light sweat, mist yourself with a spray bottle filled with water.

Professional Tip: *For longer-lasting sweat, mix one part glycerin to four parts water in your spray bottle. Be careful using it around your eyes – it can sting!*

CHAPTER 9
WITCH

From *The Wizard of Oz* to *Sleeping Beauty*, an evil **Witch** is another iconic character that you can have a lot of fun with. We're going to play with a classic green wicked witch. This makeup will be our first to incorporate basic **prosthetics** (sometimes called **appliances**), which you will use for many of your characters from this point on.

The nose and chin for this makeup are available at costume shops or Halloween stores. These hollow rubber prosthetics are inexpensive and easy to use.

STEP 1

If you're not planning to wear a black wig, spray your hair with some black temporary hair color. Clean the excess off your skin with rubbing alcohol.

If you plan to wear a wig with your makeup, pin your hair back and move on to the next step.

STEP 2

Stuff the nose and chin with cotton. This will make the prosthetics a little more solid so that they're easier to work with than they would be if left hollow and floppy.

STEP 3

Hold the nose against your skin to figure out the right placement. You may have to trim the edges a bit with scissors to get the prosthetic to fit right; just don't cut too much off. A very thick cut edge will be harder to blend smoothly into your skin.

Once you're happy with the position of the nose, powder around the edge heavily. When you remove the prosthetic, you will have bare skin showing where the nose goes. This process is called **registration** and is a handy guide for gluing.

STEP 4

Apply spirit gum to your bare skin just inside the powder registration. When the spirit gum is tacky, press the nose in place. Repeat these steps to glue on the chin. Dust away the excess powder once both prosthetics are in place.

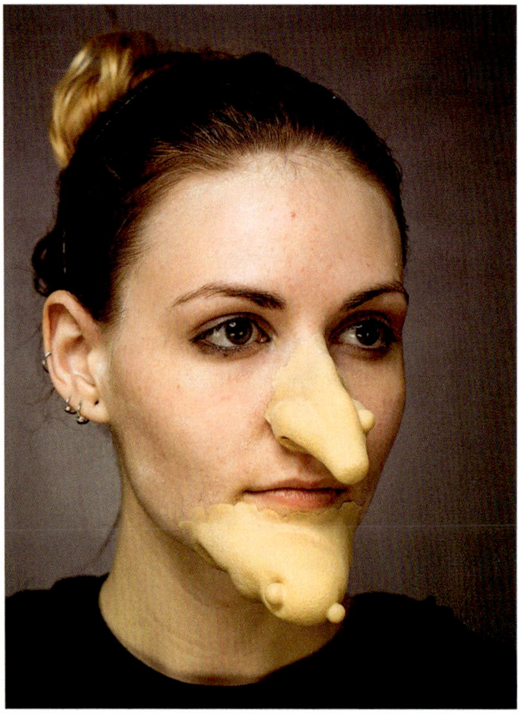

FIGURE 9.1 Step 4

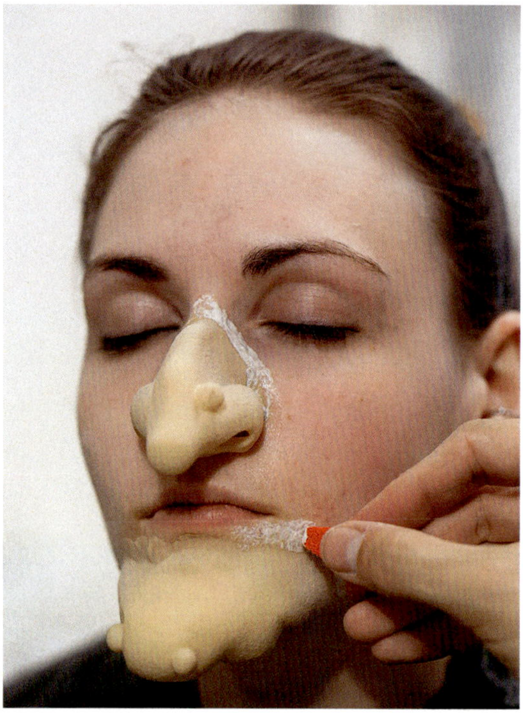

FIGURE 9.2 Step 5

STEP 5

Stipple a small amount of latex eyelash adhesive around the edges of the prosthetics. This will help them to blend more smoothly into your skin. Allow the latex to dry and then powder it. If you had to trim the edges of the prosthetic you may need more than one coat of latex to blend the thicker cut edge.

STEP 6

Mix a batch of sunburn-red RMG and apply it to the nose and chin, extending it past the edges onto the skin a bit. Powder it before moving on to the next step.

This red serves a specific purpose: it helps to simulate the warmth created by blood and muscle underneath the skin. It will make the next color match your skin more realistically; without it, the same green may read differently on your skin and the rubber.

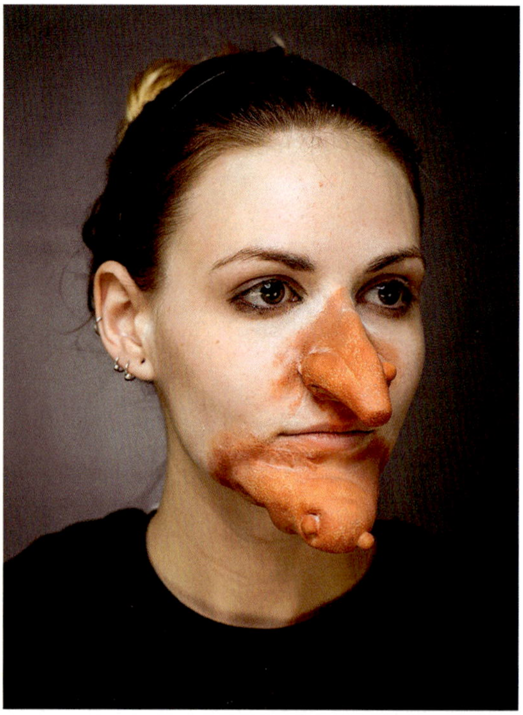

FIGURE 9.3 Step 6

FIGURE 9.4 Step 7

FIGURE 9.5 Step 9

STEP 7

Mix a batch of green RMG and stipple it onto the nose and chin, extending it out past the edges of the prosthetics onto your skin. Use regular cream makeup on the rest of your face and neck. You can skip your ears if you have a wig that hides them.

STEP 8

Powder the foundation now if you want, or wait until the highlight and shadow are applied if you prefer.

STEP 9

Add shadows to your cheeks, temples, eye area, jawline, neck and the sides of your nose with a dark grayish-green color. This is a good theatrical character, so go heavier with your shadows for a bolder effect.

Add some hard shadows to your nasolabial folds, under your eyes, in the crow's feet area

FIGURE 9.6 Step 10

and in the anger lines between your eyebrows (I missed that last one in the Step 9 photo, but they're included in the next one).

STEP 10

Add yellowish highlights on high areas (cheeks, nose, chin, etc.) to accentuate the shadows. Yellow and green are two colors that work well together, which makes sense as yellow is a component of green.

STEP 11

Paint the warts brown and then powder the makeup if you haven't already.

STEP 12

Darken your eyebrows and accentuate their pointiness. I gave them an upturn in the center to make our witch look a little meaner.

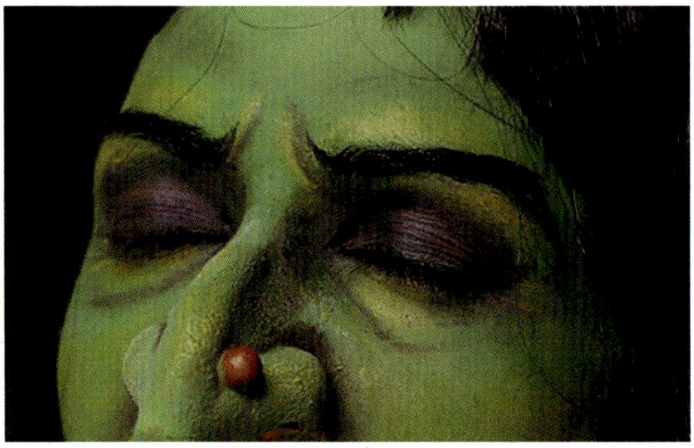

FIGURE 9.7

I also included a few beauty elements such as black lipstick, black eyeliner and purple eyeshadow. These are optional, but I wanted a witch that looks a little more glamorous.

Put on a black wig (if you have one) and a classic witch dress and hat to finish off your character.

SECTION 2

ADVANCED MATERIALS AND TECHNIQUES

Credit: Christopher Payne

CHAPTER 10
FANGS AND CLAWS

You can make your own fangs and claws out of an amazing product called thermoplastic. Several different companies make it, and you can buy it at many costume shops and craft stores. The brand I've seen most often is called Friendly Plastic.

Thermoplastic is sold either in sheets (good for costumes and cosplay) or in small pellets, which work perfectly for a makeup artist. The pellets melt to a putty consistency at about 140° F (60° C), meaning that you can dip them in hot water and make them pliable. As the plastic cools it hardens again into whatever shape you've molded it into. The best part is you can remelt it as many times as you want, so a single bag of pellets can last a long, long time.

Let's start by making some fangs for your **Vampire**.

> **Author's Note:** *You should not use this technique if you have braces or loose teeth.*

STEP 1

Heat a cup of water in a microwave until it's steaming – about the temperature of a cup of cocoa. You can also use a tea kettle if you want, but don't heat the water all the way to boiling. That's a lot hotter than you need and could result in a painful burn.

STEP 2

Pour a small pile of pellets into a spoon and then dip them slowly into the hot water. The pellets will want to float off the spoon, so take your time. I've found that dipping the edge of the spoon in the water to fill it slowly works pretty well. I use an old spoon with the handle bent up at a 90° angle for easier dipping into the cup. If you have a dedicated spoon and cup just for thermoplastic, you don't need to worry about cleaning up any escaped plastic before your next cup of coffee (a few pellets will always escape the spoon, no matter how careful you are).

The pellets will turn from white to clear when they melt, and so it's easy to tell when they're ready.

FIGURE 10.1 Thermoplastic before and after melting

Credit: Christopher Payne

STEP 3

Take the plastic out of the water and pull it off the spoon. It will be pretty warm, but so long as your water wasn't bubbling you can work with it without a problem.

STEP 4

Form the plastic blob into a shape like a candy corn with your fingers. If you have too much plastic, pull some off and set it aside for later. The goal is to make the basic shape that will become a fang.

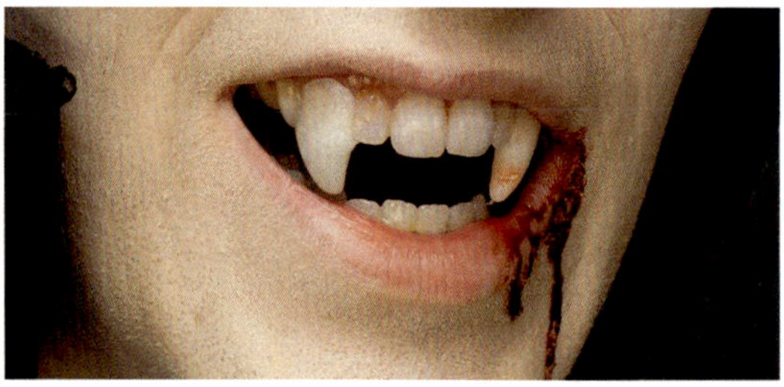

FIGURE 10.2

STEP 5

Press the fang onto one of your canine teeth. You want the plastic to cover the entire tooth, front and back. Play with the shape of the fang until you're happy with it. If your first try is no good, remelt it and try again.

STEP 6

Let the soft fang cool on your tooth for a few minutes until it turns white again. Once it does, carefully take it off and set it aside to fully harden (this takes maybe 10 minutes). Make the other fang the same way. These fangs are now custom-molded to your teeth and can pop on and off easily.

You can also use thermoplastic to make claws, following the same basic steps as for the fangs and forming each claw on an individual fingertip.

Try cutting holes in the fingertips of a glove and gluing the claws in place with hot glue. That way, you don't have to worry about losing them, and they will be easy to put on and take off as a single glove. After that, you can dress the gloves up with some cotton, latex and any additives you want (see the **Cotton and Latex** and **Skin Textures** chapters to learn how). I've made more than a few creature gloves this way.

Credit: Shutterstock

CHAPTER 11
TEETH

You can also use thermoplastic to make full sets of false teeth. Although you can buy fake teeth at costume shops, they usually don't fit very well and are only available in a few styles. These homemade teeth will be designed for your mouth, snapping right onto your own teeth, and you're only limited by your imagination.

Some stores sell thermoplastic in different colors. If you can find it, buy pink or red for the gums and white for the teeth. This will save you some painting later.

Author's Note: *As in the previous chapter, if you have a loose tooth, you should probably skip this project until it falls out and the adult tooth grows in. The same is true if you have braces.*

STEP 1

Melt enough plastic to make a rectangular sheet. It should be wide enough to wrap around the front and back of your teeth and long enough to create a new set of gums for your fake teeth. Gently press the soft, clear plastic around your teeth to form a base for the teeth and leave it in place until it turns white again.

Don't press the plastic so hard against your teeth that you can't get it off again! You can always remelt the plastic and try again if it's too loose on the first try.

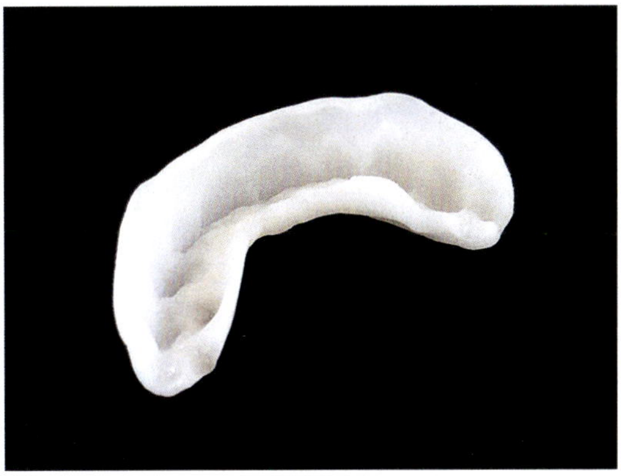

FIGURE 11.1 The inside of a completed base

STEP 2

Remove the hardened plastic base from your mouth. It may be a little tough to get it out at first as you're having to break a sort of vacuum suction, but your saliva will help the plastic come free with a little wiggling.

When you put it back onto your teeth, some edges of the base may irritate the area inside of your mouth at the very tops and bottoms of your gums. This is usually owing to the plastic oozing too far up when it was soft. Trim off any irritating edges with a sharp pair of cuticle scissors, removing a bit at a time until the base feels comfortable in your mouth. You can also shape the edges with sandpaper to remove any irritating areas.

STEP 3

Use more plastic to form the individual teeth. The shape, size and number of teeth are completely up to you, but make them a bit flatter than the fangs so you can close your mouth more easily.

STEP 4

Hold one of the teeth in a set of needle-nose pliers by the tip and soften the root end by holding it near a lighter or candle. Don't actually put the plastic into the flame or it will burn!

While the end of the tooth is molten, press it into the base section and hold it there until it cools. When the plastic solidifies, it will fuse the tooth to the base. Repeat this process for all of the teeth, one at a time (Figure 11.2).

You might be tempted to use super glue, but that stuff isn't very safe to have in your mouth even after it's dried.

STEP 5

Roll some melted plastic into a flattened snake shape and then apply it to the gum area above the teeth and smooth it out. The goal here is to create a more natural gum line, rather than teeth

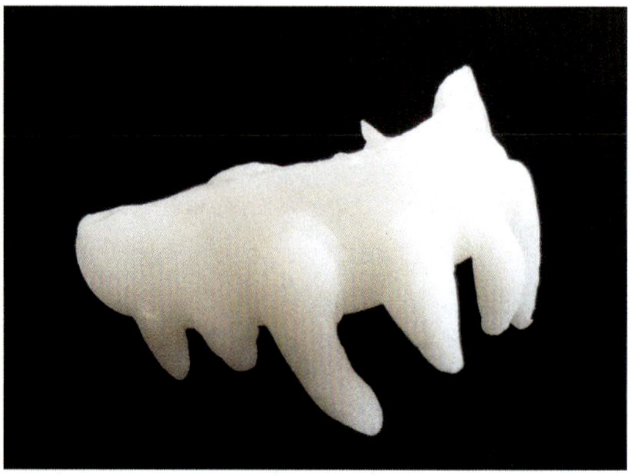

FIGURE 11.2 The base with teeth

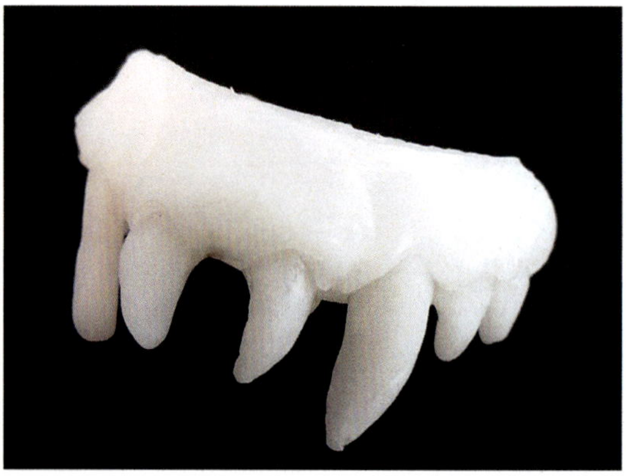

FIGURE 11.3 Gums added

just sticking out of the base. Look at your own teeth for reference if you need to.

This process works best using snakes just large enough for one or two teeth at a time. They must be applied immediately after coming out of the hot water; waiting even 20 seconds will let the plastic cool enough that it might not stick to the base.

STEP 6

Paint the teeth with acrylic paint, using a reddish-pink for the gums and ivory for the teeth (unless your character calls for something different). Once you have the base coat in place, you can thin the paint with water to apply additional washes of color to create shadows, yellowing and any other details you want.

When you're happy with the paint, allow it to dry overnight before you take your new teeth out for a test drive.

FIGURE 11.4 Ready for my closeup!

Credit: Christopher Payne

CHAPTER 12
BLOOD

Blood is a major part of any horror or gore makeup. Just adding blood to a character can push your makeup from bland to gruesome. There are many varieties of fake blood that you can buy in costume shops, but you can make your own for much less money. These blood recipes can be made with items from the grocery store. As they're food-based, they can be safely used in your mouth and on your face. You should store them in the refrigerator to keep them from spoiling and throw them away after a week or so.

Homemade blood can stain your skin, but you can remove most of the staining by covering it with Barbasol shaving cream (not gel) for a few minutes. The cream pulls the red stain back out of your skin. I don't know why it works, but it works! It's been a secret weapon of makeup artists for decades.

If you need blood that can wash out of clothing, try mixing in 25% clear liquid hand soap. This will help the blood to rinse out, but makes it unsafe to use in your mouth or near your eyes. Even with the soap, you should do a test on a small fabric swatch before soaking your best shirt.

Most fake bloods have three main components: a **vehicle**, which is the main ingredient, **pigment** to add color and an **opacifier** to make the blood more opaque and harder to see through.

Some bloods skip the opacifier, and boy does it show when it looks like you've got cherry cough syrup on your face. To show you what I mean, let's start with a recipe that's just the vehicle and pigment.

BASIC RECIPE

- 16 oz clear corn syrup
- 1 oz red food coloring
- 1 teaspoon yellow food coloring
- 1 drop blue food coloring

This is the most basic fake blood that you can make. Just mix the corn syrup and food coloring together in a bowl. Boom, done.

Because this blood does not use an opacifier (the corn syrup is the vehicle, and the food coloring is the pigment), it's pretty bright and transparent. It works well when you want it to be obvious that the blood is fake, or if it will be seen in the dark and needs to be brighter to still look red through the gloom.

Adding to the same batch, let's include an opacifier to make your blood a bit more realistic.

RECIPE 2

- 16 oz clear corn syrup
- 1 oz red food coloring
- 1 teaspoon yellow food coloring
- 1 drop blue food coloring
- 2 tablespoons hot water
- 1 tablespoon baking cocoa powder

Make the basic blood and set the bowl aside. In a separate bowl, mix the hot water and cocoa powder (hot water will dissolve the powder more easily). Stir this mixture into the blood.

The blood will now be more opaque against your skin. It will also be darker, more like real blood. If you want your blood to be a brighter red but still opaque, leave out the blue food coloring.

You can experiment with different amounts and colors of pigment for different effects. Green alien blood is no different than the stuff you just made except for the color.

PASTE BLOOD

Paste blood is a great way to make easy scabs and to add some extra punch inside your wounds. To make it, mix a tablespoon of your fake blood with coffee grounds. You want enough coffee to turn the blood into a thick paste. Don't use instant coffee – it will just dissolve and you'll loose your texture!

Once the paste is mixed, spread it onto your skin for some nasty scabs.

You can also use cornstarch to make a blood paste that's almost thick enough to sculpt with. Be aware that the cornstarch is white and will really lighten the color of your blood, so you should add extra pigment to compensate.

Author's Note: I'm of the opinion that less is more when it comes to blood. I've seen so many cool makeups completely lost in a sea of red. Usually, I like to work with a few different thicknesses of blood. I'll start dressing a makeup with something more watery before adding drips and blobs of thicker stuff here and there. The variety looks a lot more interesting than just a big red smear.

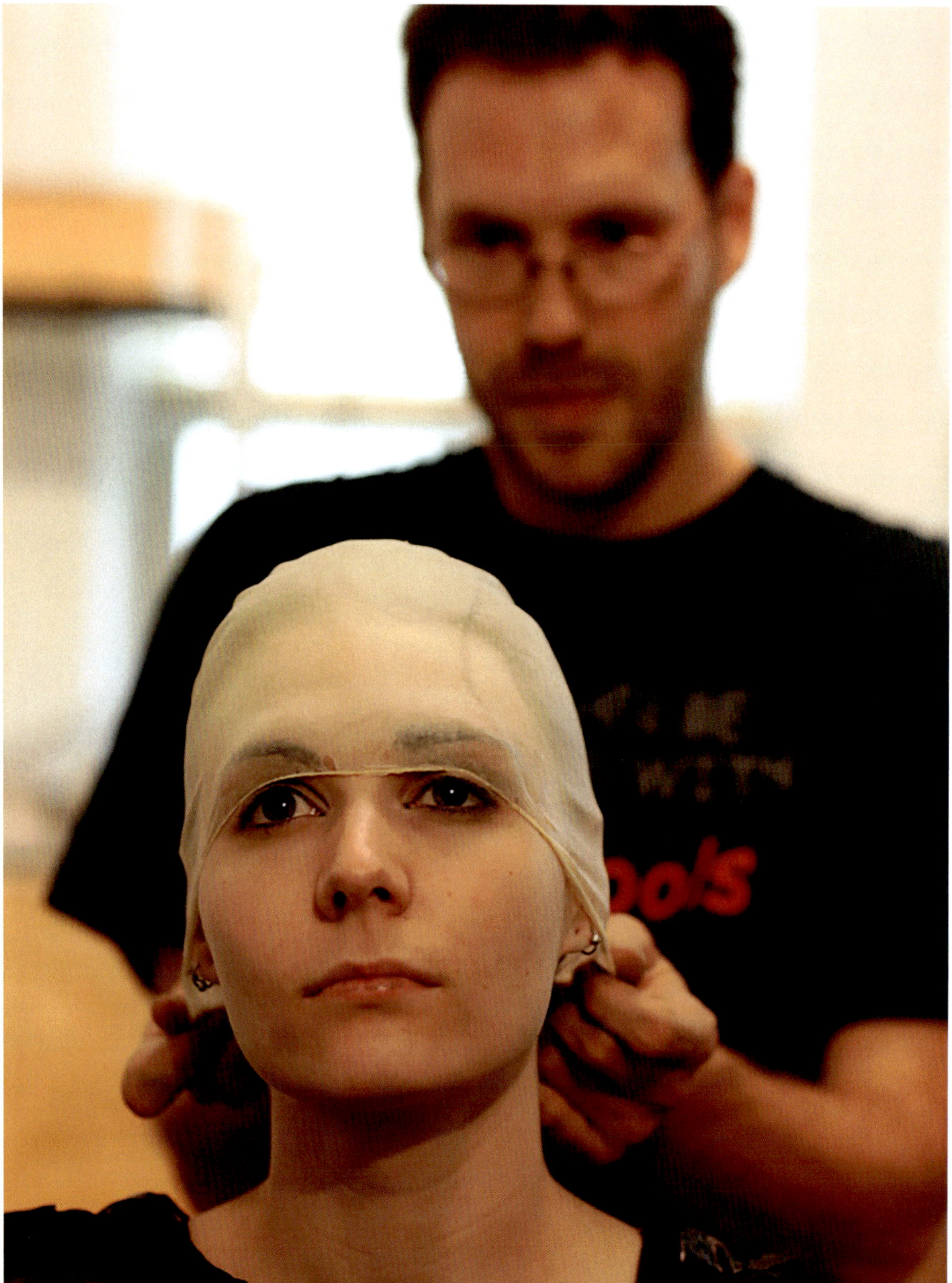

CHAPTER 13
BALD CAPS

A **bald cap** is a special kind of prosthetic that covers your hair and makes you look like you've gone bald! Latex is the most common material you'll find in costume shops, and it's what we'll be using for this book. Costume shops usually carry bald caps in a few different sizes. Make sure you pick a size that fits you well; it'll be a lot harder to apply if it's too large or too small. It should have to stretch just a bit for a nice snug fit.

Bald caps can be a bit tricky to apply on yourself. It can be done, but this is one area where it's easier to have a friend helping.

STEP 1

Slick back your hair with alcohol-free hair gel (gel containing alcohol can eat little holes in the latex). If you have long hair, pull it back into a low ponytail and braid it down your back, using multiple hair ties to keep everything nice and tight.

Once this is done, put on a rubber bald cap. It should be tight enough to fit snugly, but not so tight that it squeezes your brain until you pass out. Chances are it will come down way too far – that's normal for generic caps.

STEP 2

Draw a line on the cap following your hairline with a makeup pencil. This line should be about an inch

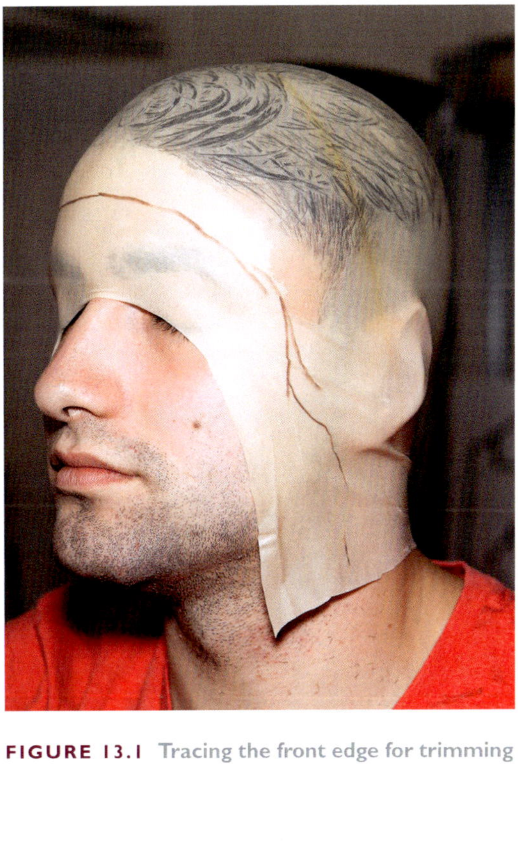

FIGURE 13.1 Tracing the front edge for trimming

below your hairline on the front and sides and will give you a cutting guide for the next step. Don't worry about the ears or the back of the neck yet.

STEP 3

Take the cap off and trim along the line with a sharp pair of scissors. Carefully put the cap back on once you've finished.

STEP 4

Flip the edges of the bald cap up to expose the skin underneath. This gives you room to apply the glue.

STEP 5

Apply a thin coat of spirit gum along your forehead where the cap will lie. Tap it with your finger to get it tacky, then press the bald cap in place. The glue line should extend about a half-inch from your hairline; any cap beyond that will be trimmed away later.

STEP 6

Glue the cap down behind your neck. You may need a friend to help with this part, or you can try working in a mirror. Look up slightly while you're doing this so that the cap will stretch tight when you look forward again. Otherwise the cap will bulge out at the neck every time you look up.

If you have longer hair in a braid, you will have to glue the cap down to either side and leave the middle open so your hair can pass through. This hair must be covered with a costume, but it's worth it to ensure that your

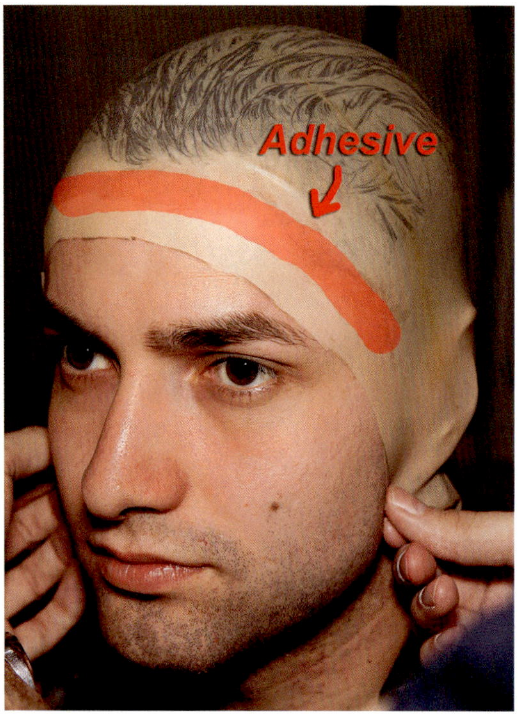

FIGURE 13.2 Gluing the front of the cap

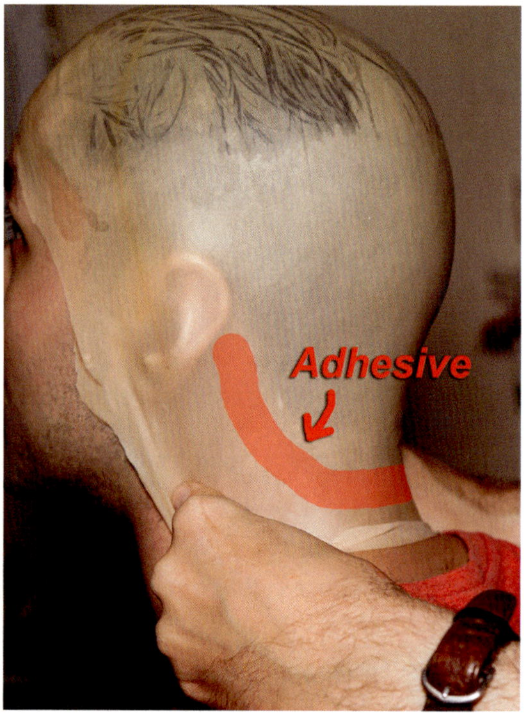

FIGURE 13.3 Gluing the back of the cap

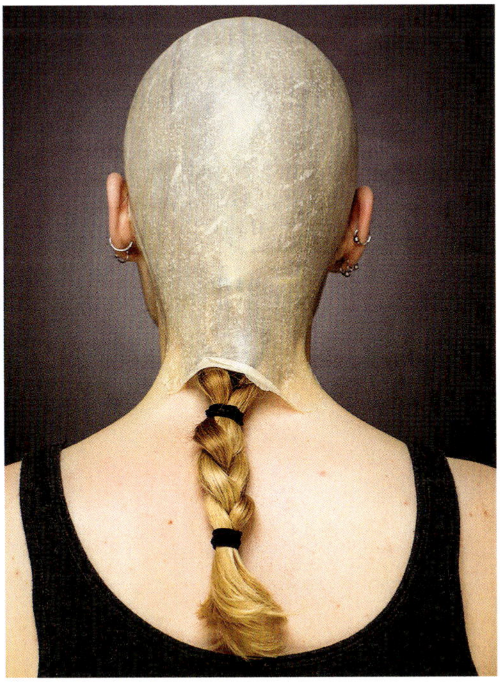

FIGURE 13.4 Bald cap with long hair

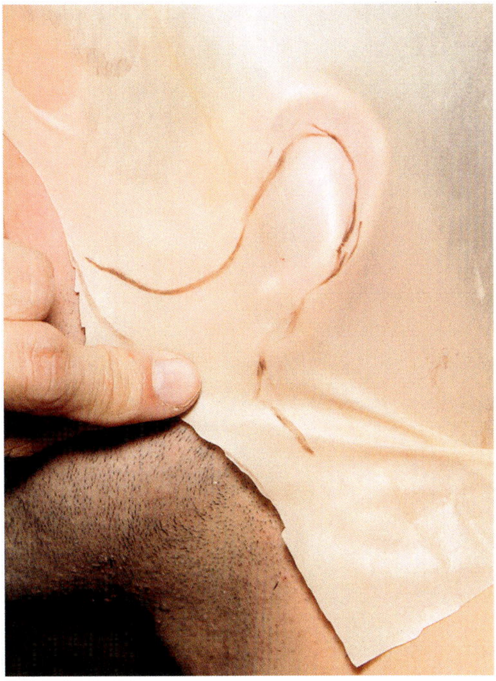

FIGURE 13.5 Sketching on the ear trim line

bald head is as smooth as possible. It's possible to cram a lot of hair under a bald cap, but keeping the surface from looking lumpy can be a real challenge.

STEP 7

Draw a line on the cap about a quarter-inch inside the ear, extending it below the sideburn area and down the side of the neck. It will be like an upside-down U. Carefully cut this section out using a pair of rounded cuticle scissors (small scissors with a rounded tip so you don't poke yourself).

STEP 8

Pop your ear out of the U-shape and see how smoothly the cap lies around your ear. You may have to trim the top and front corner a bit to

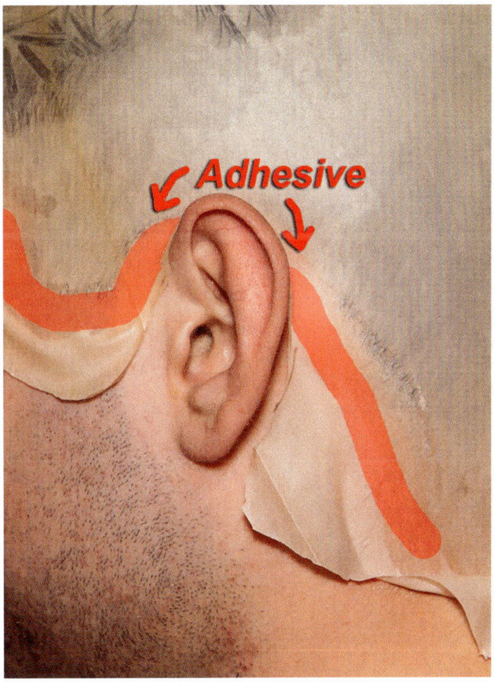

FIGURE 13.6 Gluing around the ear

prevent a wrinkle from forming above the ear. Cut away a tiny bit at a time until the cap fits over your ear smoothly.

STEP 9

Glue down the cap in front of your ear first and then glue behind your ear. You're doing behind the ear last because, if there are any little wrinkles from the cap not fitting perfectly, this is the best place to hide them.

STEP 10

Repeat the previous step for your other ear.

There is another way of doing the ears on a bald cap, called the "birthing method." Basically, you cut a hole in the side of the bald cap about the size of a quarter (see Figure 13.7) and then pop your ear through it. While this does give you more surface to glue, I'm not a fan of the technique for two reasons: I feel it doesn't give you as much control over the fit of your cap, and it can get a little tight and uncomfortable on the ear after a while.

As with most things in the makeup biz, there's more than one way of doing things. Give it a try and, if you like it better than the method I've used, go for it!

STEP 11

Go back around the entire cap and trim away the excess rubber and then glue down any final loose edges.

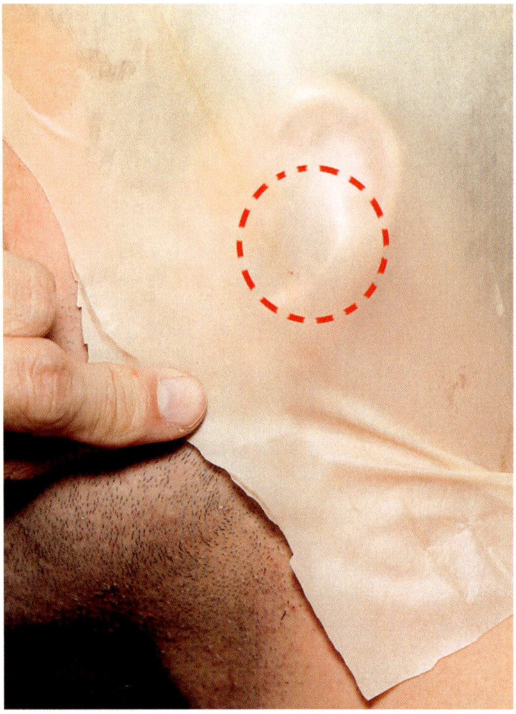

FIGURE 13.7 The hole used to expose your ear with the birthing method

Author's Note: *As you get more skilled with bald caps, you can use a thinner line of glue and trim the edge closer and closer to your hairline so less cap shows on your skin. You should never trim closer than a quarter-inch below your hairline or the glue won't have a strong enough hold.*

STEP 12

Stipple a coat or two of latex eyelash adhesive around the edges of the cap to help blend it into your skin, the same way you did with the Witch prosthetics. Powder the latex once you're done.

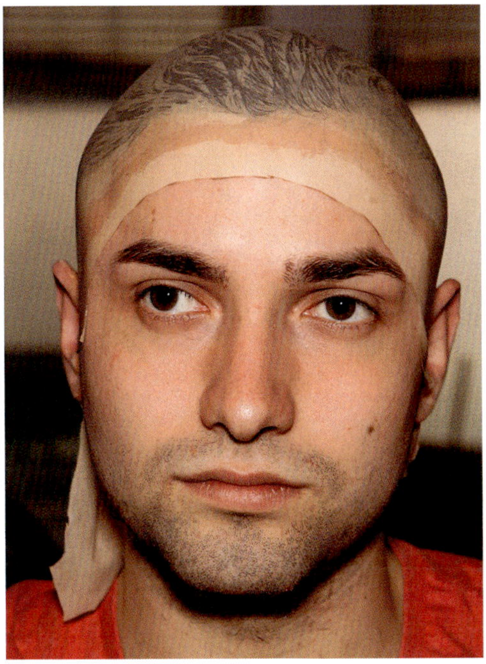

FIGURE 13.8 Bald cap edges before final trimming

FIGURE 13.10 The finished bald cap with makeup

FIGURE 13.9 Edges after final trimming

STEP 13

Apply sunburn-red RMG to the entire cap and then powder it and apply RMG that matches the skin color of your character. You can also stipple dark makeup to look like the stubble left behind by a freshly shaved head or apply real hair following the procedure listed in the **Hair and Stubble** chapter.

Everyone in a bald cap seemed to have the same character in mind ...

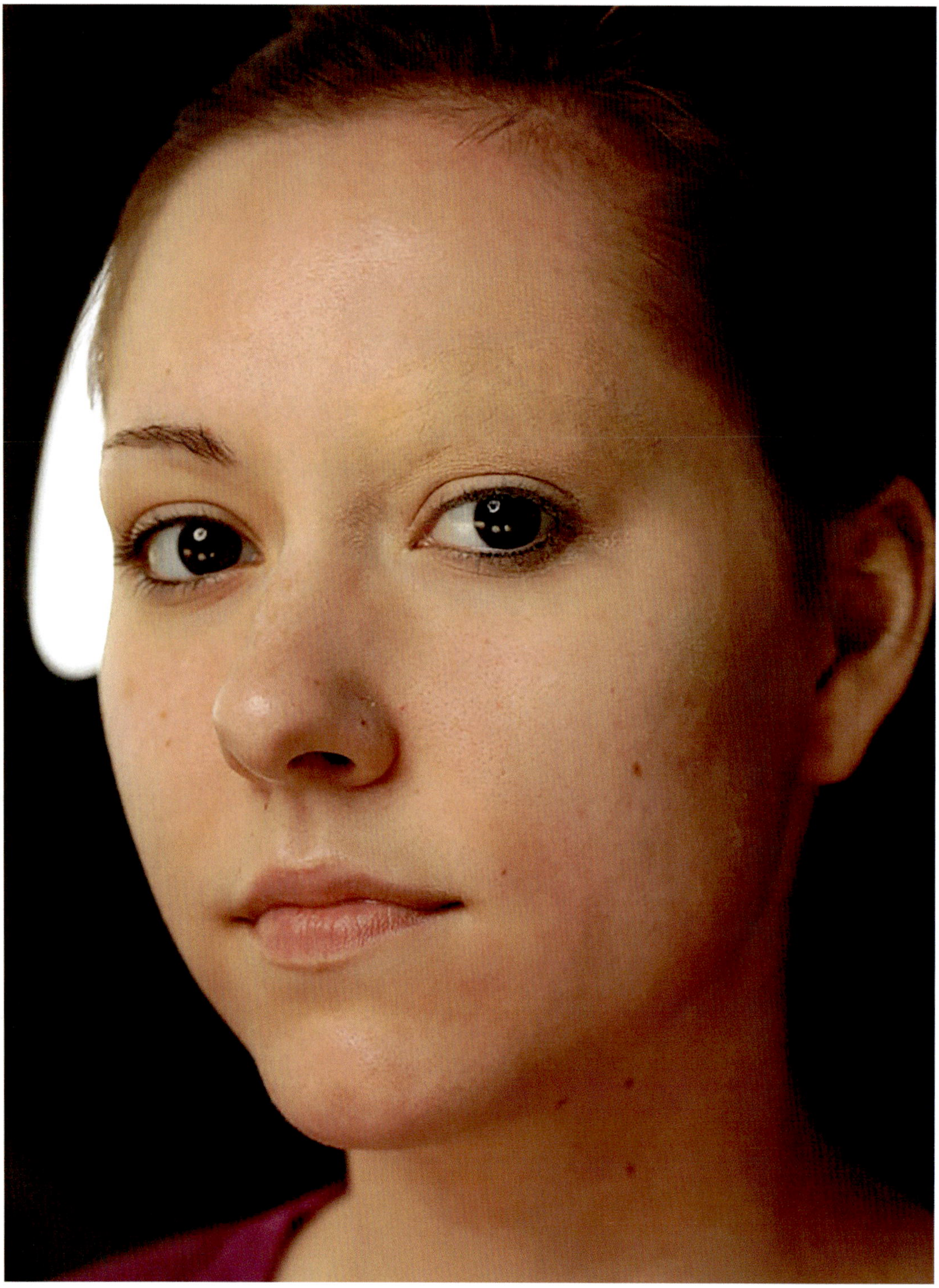

CHAPTER 14

BLOCKING OUT HAIR

Sometimes you may want to hide your eyebrows for a character. This is often most easily done by gluing a small bit of rubber over the eyebrow (such as a scrap of bald cap or a piece of a rubber glove), but you can also block out hair with a bar of soap, nose putty or a washable glue stick.

STEP 1

Place a small bar of soap (like the kind you get in a hotel) in a glass containing an inch of water. The soap needs to soak until it develops a slimy film on the surface.

If you're using nose putty or a glue stick, you can obviously skip this step.

STEP 2

Rub the soap, putty or glue stick against the hair you want to block out. If your eyebrows are thick, you may need to spread the hairs out as much as you can against your skin, rubbing the soap or glue in every direction. It will look a little silly, but that won't matter once it's covered with makeup.

The goal is to get the hair as flat against your skin as possible. Don't just do one pass and call it done or you'll end up with a lumpy texture that is easy to spot.

STEP 3

Let the soap or glue completely dry. You can speed this up with a hairdryer if you want.

STEP 4

Brush a coat of spirit gum onto the glue or soap to secure it in place, letting it dry before adding makeup. Seal nose putty with liquid latex instead of spirit gum.

STEP 5

Cover the hair with sunburn-red makeup and then a foundation that matches your character's skin color.

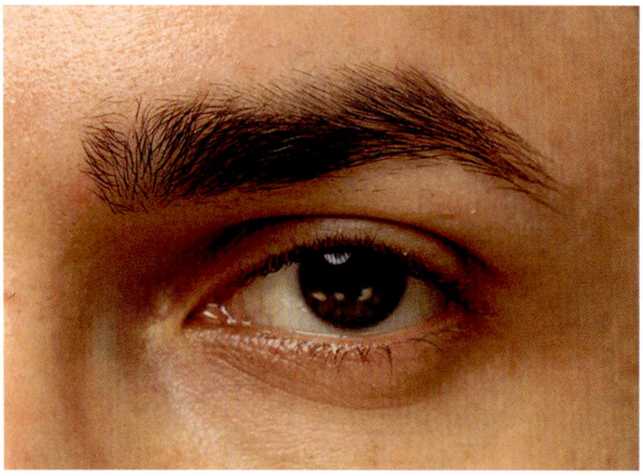

FIGURE 14.1 Uncovered eyebrow

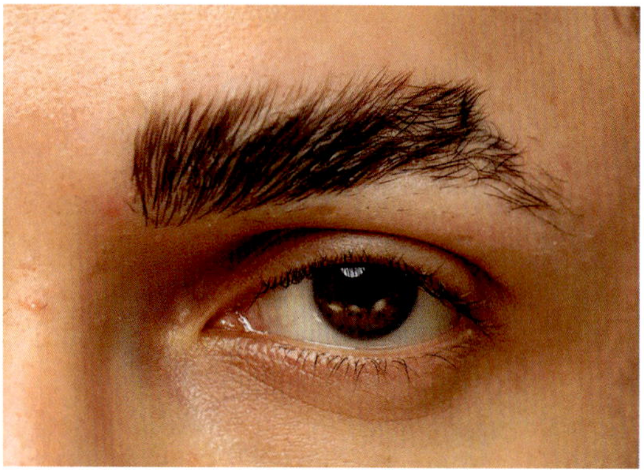

FIGURE 14.2 Hairs adhered to skin

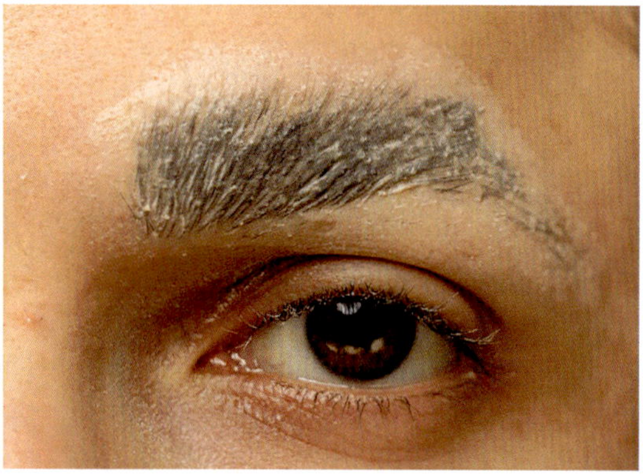

FIGURE 14.3 Latex added

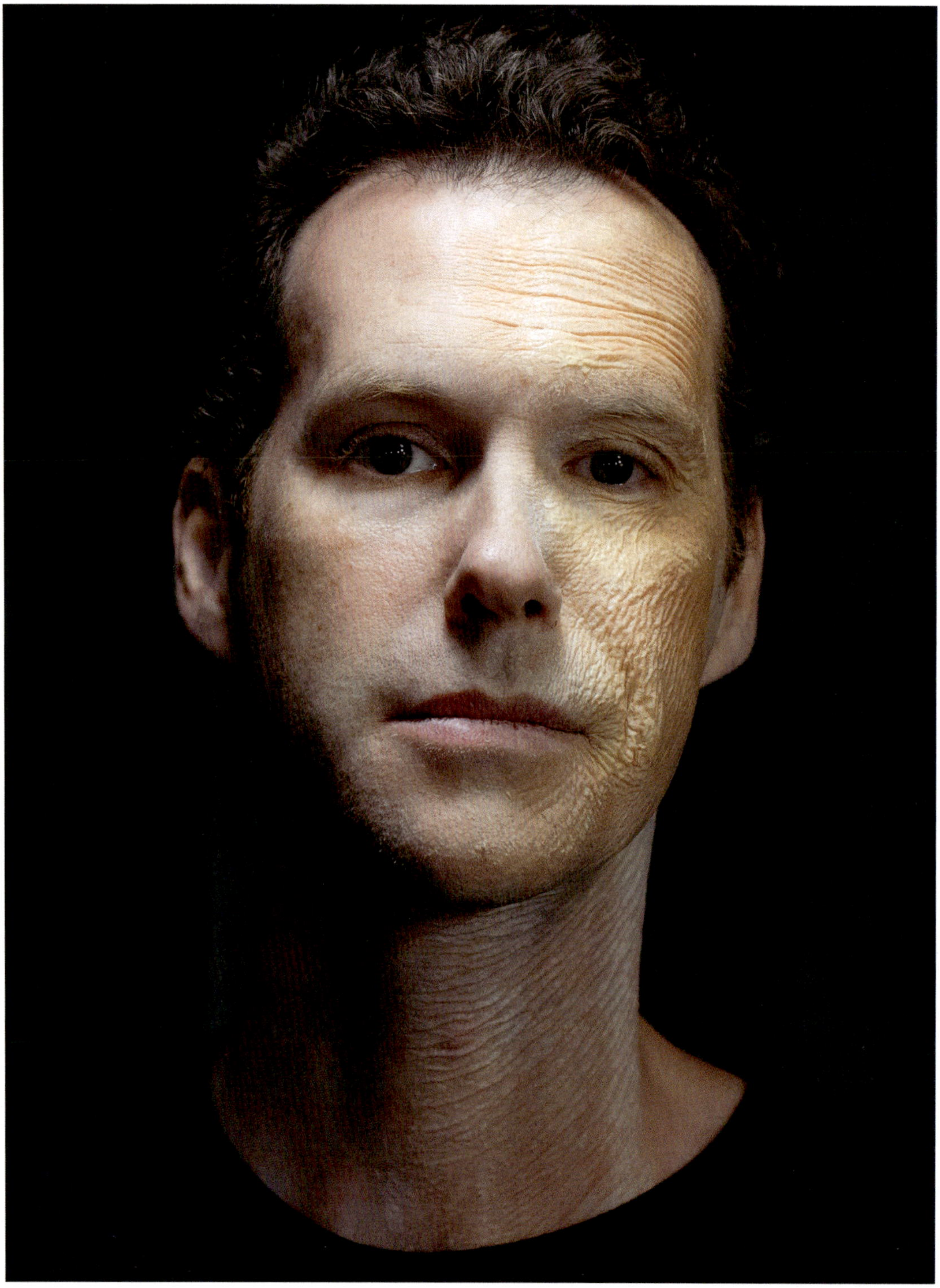

Credit: Christopher Payne

CHAPTER 15
SKIN TEXTURES

Many creature makeups may not work well with your natural skin. After all, if you're going to be a rotting zombie or beastie that's been living under a rock, you don't want a flawless complexion to diminish the effect. There are a lot of ways you can create different **skin textures** using makeup.

COLOR ONLY

The easiest way to add texture to the skin is just to paint it on. For characters such as the **Pirate** and **Basic Zombie**, you stippled on color to create an irregular skin texture. This can be taken to an extreme by using a natural sea sponge or oversized paint brush to do the stippling, creating large variations in the application. With multiple overlapping layers of texture, you can add a lot of interesting surface detail. This type of large-scale texture works well with pancake makeup, but you can also get the same results by thinning down cream makeup with either hand lotion or rubbing alcohol.

Another neat coloring technique that I use all the time is called **spattering**. Cut the bristles of a 1-inch paint brush (the cheap kind from a hardware store) down to about a ½-inch above the metal part. Thin some cream makeup with rubbing alcohol and then use the cut brush to apply it by flicking the bristles with your fingers, creating an irregular spatter pattern on your skin. Use this technique to build up layers of different-colored skin tones for a more subtle effect than you get with the sea sponge.

LATEX AND ADDITIVES

We've already covered building out facial features with cotton and latex. But latex is a material that you can use to create a lot of skin textures as well! To do this, apply a layer of liquid latex to your face. While it's wet, press one of the following additives into the latex:

- Bread crumbs
- Corn flakes

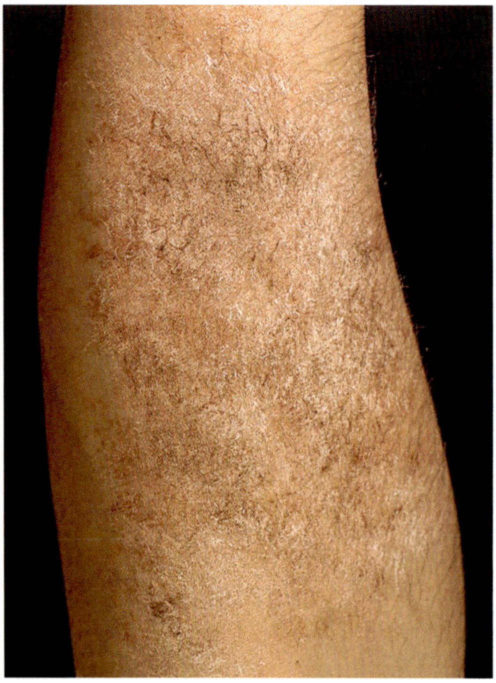

FIGURE 15.1 Skin texture with color only

FIGURE 15.2 Spattering shades of blue onto an alien character

- Oatmeal
- Dry rice
- Puffed rice cereal
- Cracker meal
- Anything else with an interesting texture

Any of these can provide a great skin texture. You can apply these either by filling a bowl and pressing handfuls against your face or by loading a folded paper towel or powder puff and pressing the whole thing against your face.

Once the latex has dried and fully glued the additive in place, gently brush away any excess that didn't stick completely and apply a second layer of latex on top to seal it in. You can apply another layer of additive to build up even more texture, repeating the process as many times as you want. Once you are done, let the final top coat of latex dry and powder.

If you build up enough layers, you may end up with a makeup that's thick enough to be peeled off in one piece and used as a mask! You'll see an example of this toward the end of the book. You can also see an example at the start of the **Fangs and Claws** chapter. That monster hand was textured with latex and dried oatmeal flakes, applied to an opera glove instead of the skin to create a costume piece.

GELATIN

The same gelatin you created boils with can be applied directly to your skin to create some pretty

FIGURE 15.3 Applying the additive

FIGURE 15.4 Latex and bread crumbs texture

weird textures. You can prepare the gelatin the same way as you did for the boils, but stir it until it gets a little cooler before you put it on your skin. **Steaming hot gelatin can cause serious burns if you're not careful!**

You can either smooth the gelatin onto your skin and apply an additive (an alternative to using latex) or keep tapping it with a craft stick as it cools to get a stringy texture. This texture is good for burns (see an example in the **Severe Burn** chapter) and scars, depending on how you color it. Keep gooping the gelatin around your face until you're happy with it.

> **Professional Tip:** *Gelatin is one material that you absolutely CAN get in your hair! Because it melts, you can hop into a hot shower and let it dissolve away.*

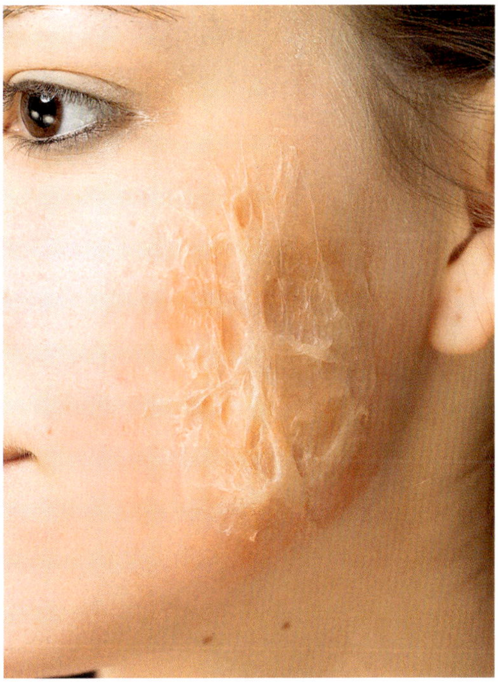

FIGURE 15.5 Gelatin burn scar

You can add additional layers of gelatin if you want, or even use cotton batting to do buildups using the same technique as with latex (see next section).

If the gelatin is slightly sticky when it dries on your skin, powder it before you add makeup.

LATEX AND TISSUE OR PAPER TOWELS

Latex can be used to adhere either tissues or paper towels to your skin, creating a wrinkled, leathery effect. Tissues provide a more realistic skin texture, whereas paper towels work better for creature skin. Whether you use tissues or paper towels, make sure they don't have any texture.

Begin by ripping the cut edges off the tissues or towels. You're doing this because irregular edges are easier to blend into each other and your skin than straight ones.

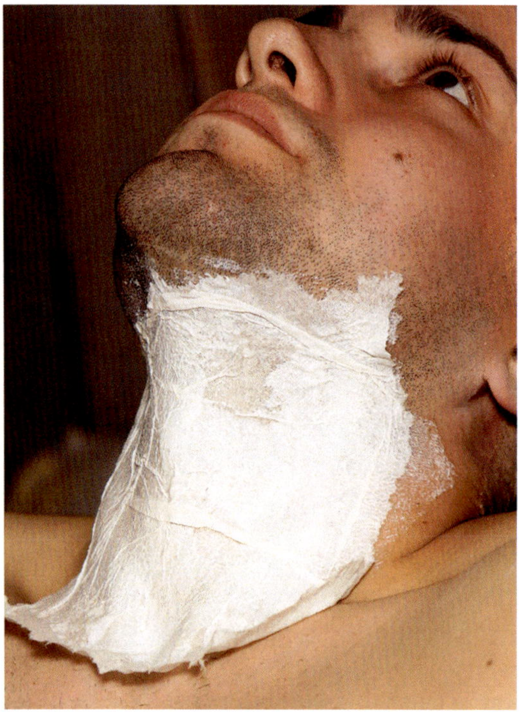

FIGURE 15.6 **Skin stretched while latex is drying**

FIGURE 15.7 **Resulting texture**

Apply a layer of latex onto your skin and then press a section of tissue or towel into it. For extra texture, wad it up first, then smooth it out before pressing it in place. Apply another layer of latex on top to seal the tissue or towel in place. You can add additional sections of tissue or towel with a slight overlap to cover as much of your skin as you want. You can also build up multiple layers of latex and tissue for heavier texture. Several examples of this technique appear later in the book.

For a really extreme wrinkling effect, you can stretch your skin in the opposite direction to the wrinkles during the application (see Figures 15.6 and 15.7). For example, for horizontal neck wrinkles, you would tip your head back to stretch the skin vertically while you apply the latex and tissue.

Once you have finished, powder the latex to keep it from sticking to itself before releasing the stretch. Your skin will try to spring back in place, but the latex and tissue will cause wrinkles to form.

You can also use this technique with just latex for a more subtle effect known as stretch and stipple. It's a method that's been used by makeup artists to create old-age characters for decades, from Don Corleone in *The Godfather* to the spellbound Theoden in *Lord of the Rings: The Two Towers*. The image at the start of this chapter shows stretch and stipple applied to half of my face.

For this technique to work, you need to stretch your skin in the opposite direction to the intended wrinkles. This can be a bit tricky to think about at first, so Figures 15.8–15.16 show the directions you want to follow as you apply the latex (add tissue for extreme wrinkling). You can do these stretches on yourself one-handed, but it can be really helpful to have a friend apply the latex while you hold the stretch (remember to powder before you let go).

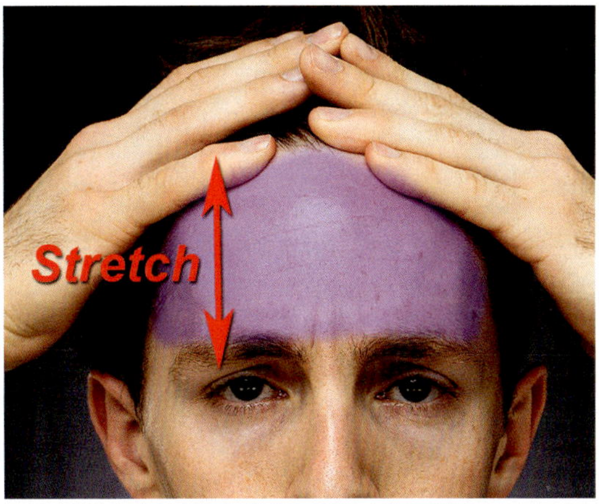

FIGURE 15.8 Forehead: Stretch up (furrow your eyebrows down to maximize the stretch)

> **Professional Tip:** *Because the ammonia fumes from liquid latex can irritate your eyes, try using latex eyelash adhesive in those sensitive areas. The adhesive has almost no ammonia and is much more comfortable around the eyes.*

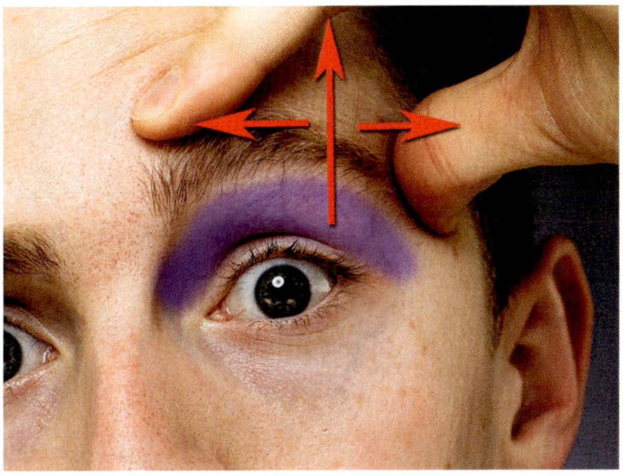

FIGURE 15.9 Above the eye: Use your thumb and index finger to pull the eyebrow up, then spread the fingers to stretch out at the same time

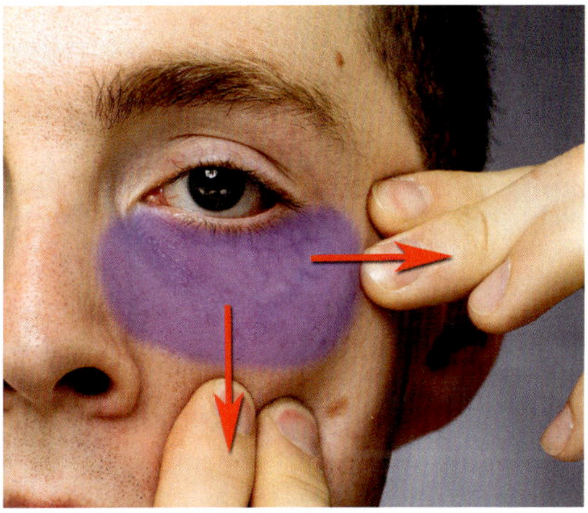

FIGURE 15.10 Below the eye: Stretch down under the eye and out from the side at the same time

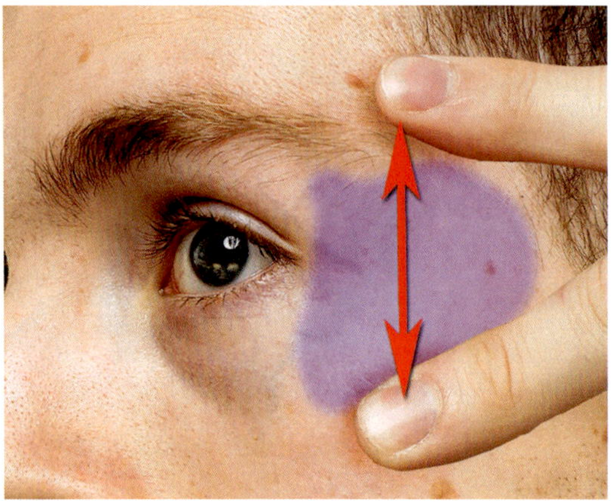

FIGURE 15.11 Crow's feet: Stretch the skin beside your eye up and down at the same time

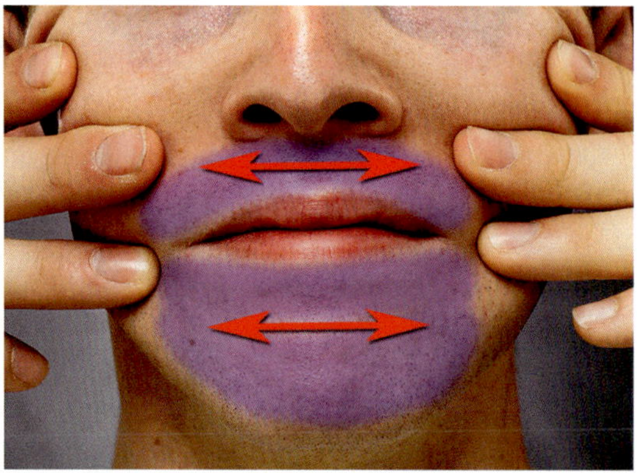

FIGURE 15.12 Upper lip, lower lip and chin: Stretch sideways in both directions at the same time. Do the upper lip and lower lip–chin area separately for better control

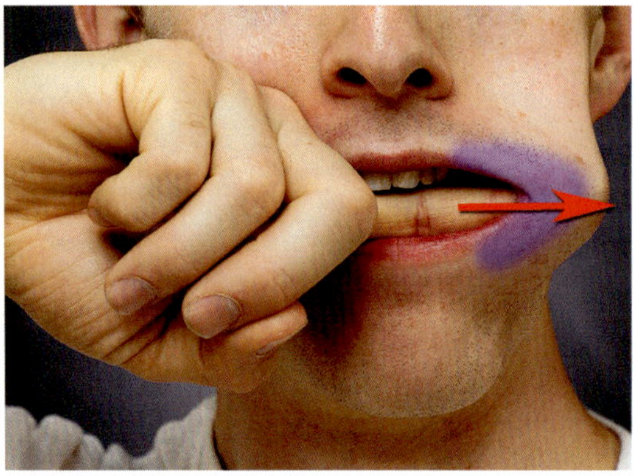

FIGURE 15.13 Corners of mouth: Use your finger to push your cheek out sideways while you apply the latex. Repeat for the other side when the first side is done

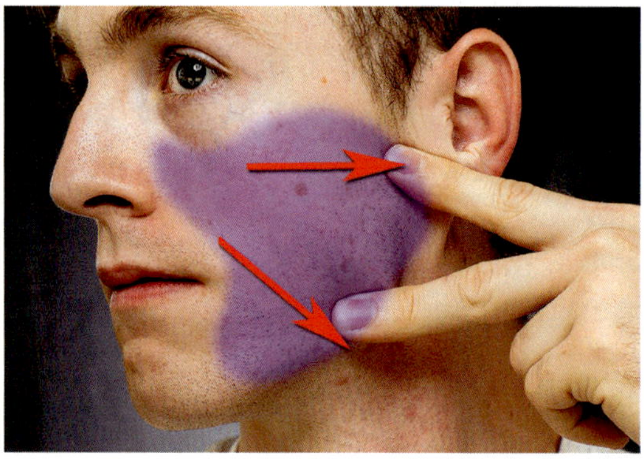

FIGURE 15.14 Cheeks: Stretch the skin back and down at the same time. Finish one cheek before doing the other

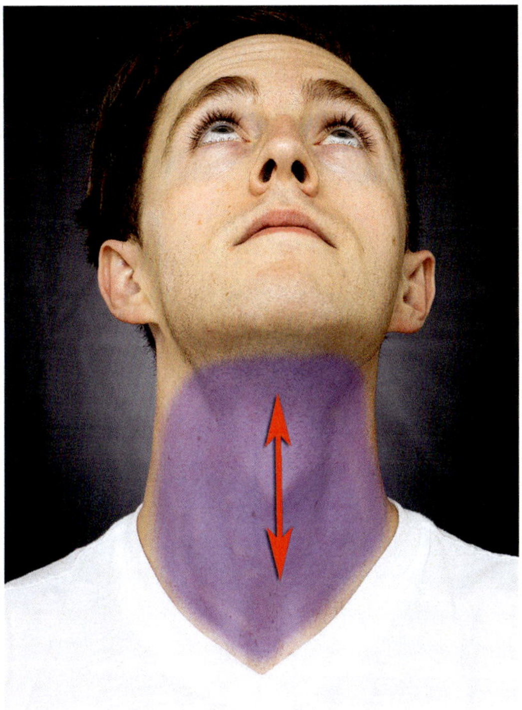

FIGURE 15.15 Front of neck: Tilt your head back as far as you can comfortably

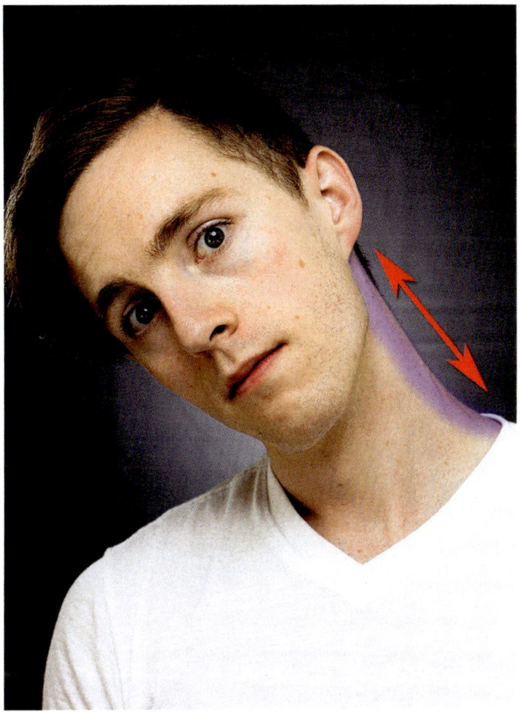

FIGURE 15.16 Sides of neck: Tilt your head as far to the side as you can comfortably. Do each side separately

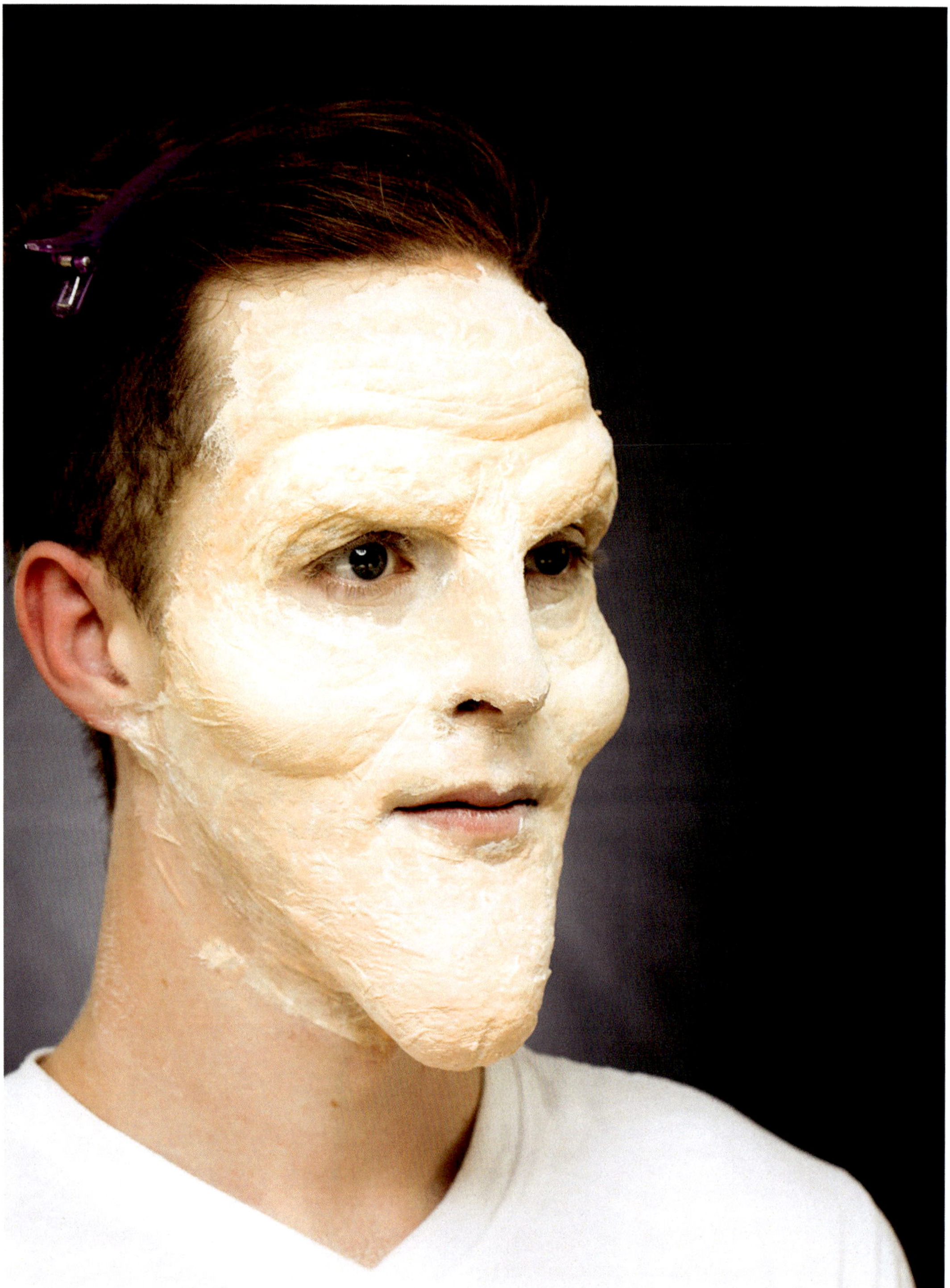

CHAPTER 16
COTTON AND LATEX

The **cotton and latex** buildup is a technique of adding layers of material onto your skin to change its shape. It's a classic method for creating monsters, though not really used professionally anymore because premade prosthetics (such as the **Witch**'s nose and chin) have made the process obsolete. Still, I think it's a lot of fun and a good trick for any makeup artist to have in their back pocket.

STEP 1

Pull apart some cotton batting into strips. Cotton balls can be used in a pinch, but they don't work nearly as well. It's worth a visit to a fabric store to get some good batting that you can tear into strips.

STEP 2

Brush some liquid latex onto your skin where you want to build up the surface. If it's going over hair such as your eyebrows, first protect the hair with a thin coat of nose putty. Apply the latex to an area slightly larger than the buildup will be.

STEP 3

Press a piece of cotton into the wet latex. This first layer of cotton shouldn't extend past the edges of the wet latex. It will give you a base to build up shapes on.

STEP 4

Lightly brush more liquid latex on top of the cotton base to seal it in place.

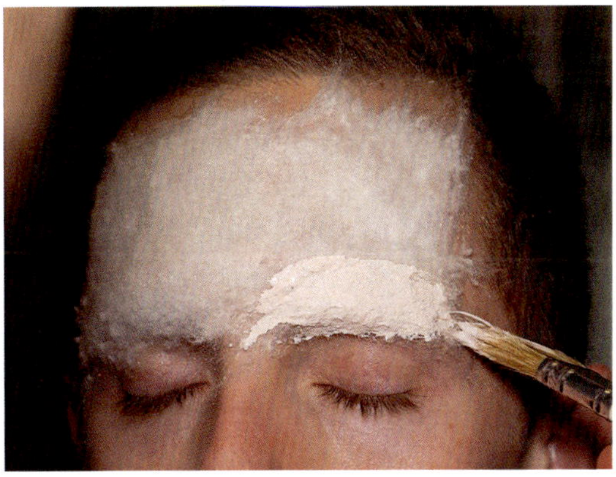

FIGURE 16.1 Step 4

STEP 5

Add more layers of cotton and latex to build up bigger shapes. These layers don't have to be flat: tubes, balls, wads and other shapes can quickly build up bulk. Once the shape is right, apply a final flat layer of cotton and latex to act as the outer surface. This final layer should blend into your skin.

You can use a popsicle stick or art spatula to adjust the shape and to sculpt heavy wrinkles and other details while the latex is wet. Things may be a bit stringy and rough right now, but that's okay. You're going to fix that in the next step. Once you're happy, let the latex dry.

Try not to completely saturate the inner layers of cotton with liquid latex as that will just

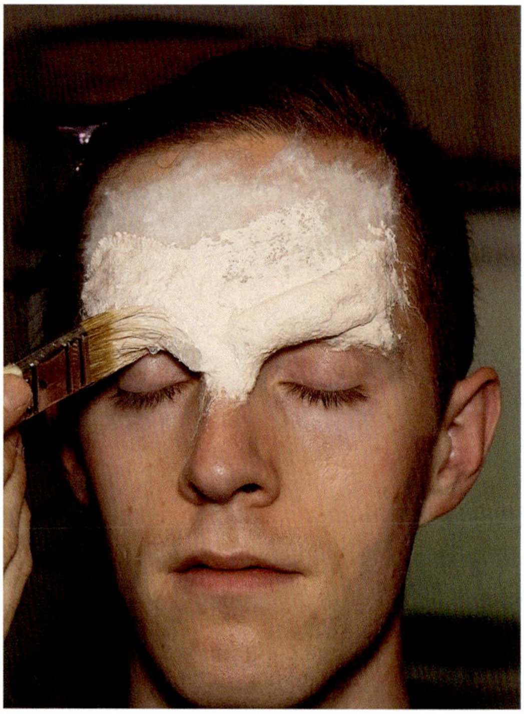

FIGURE 16.3 Step 5 (in progress)

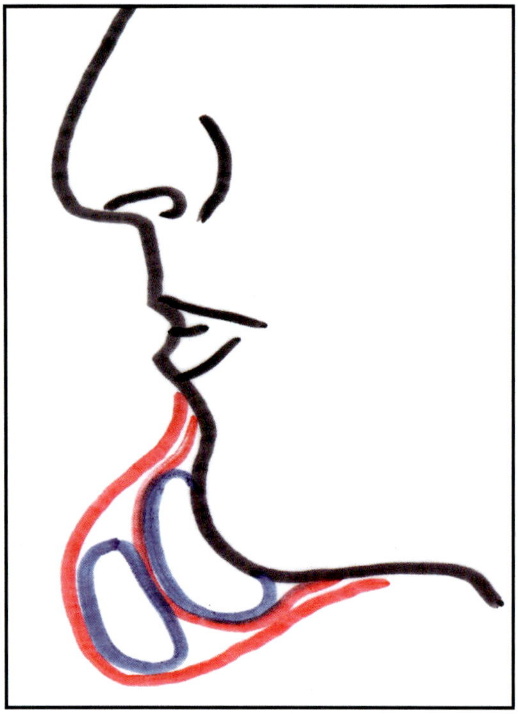

FIGURE 16.2 Building up a larger structure with alternating **wads** and **flat layers**

Credit: Christopher Payne

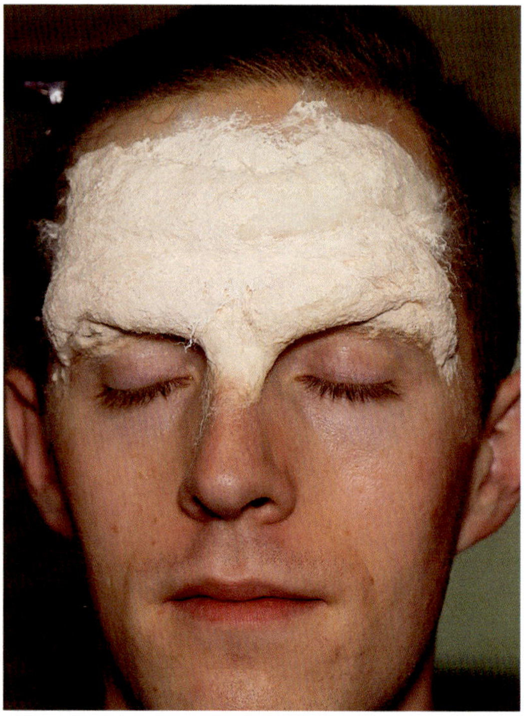

FIGURE 16.4 Step 5 (complete)

make the finished buildup heavier and much slower to dry. All you need the latex to do is stick the cotton in place and seal the outer layer.

STEP 6

Apply a unified skin to the buildup using tissue and latex. This skin can be smooth or wrinkled, depending on your character, but as before you should tear the edges to help them blend into your skin. Overlap smaller pieces as needed, just like you did for creating skin textures. You can sculpt additional fine wrinkles into the latex-soaked tissue if you want.

Let the latex on the surface dry before moving on to the final step.

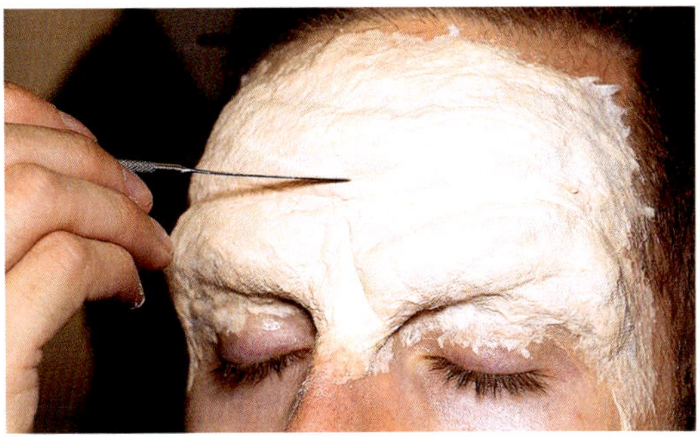

FIGURE 16.5 Step 6

STEP 7

Powder the dry latex to keep it from sticking to itself and then use RMG for your foundation.

Cotton and latex buildups can be done right on your face or in advance on a plastic face form and peeled off to create a simple, reusable prosthetic.

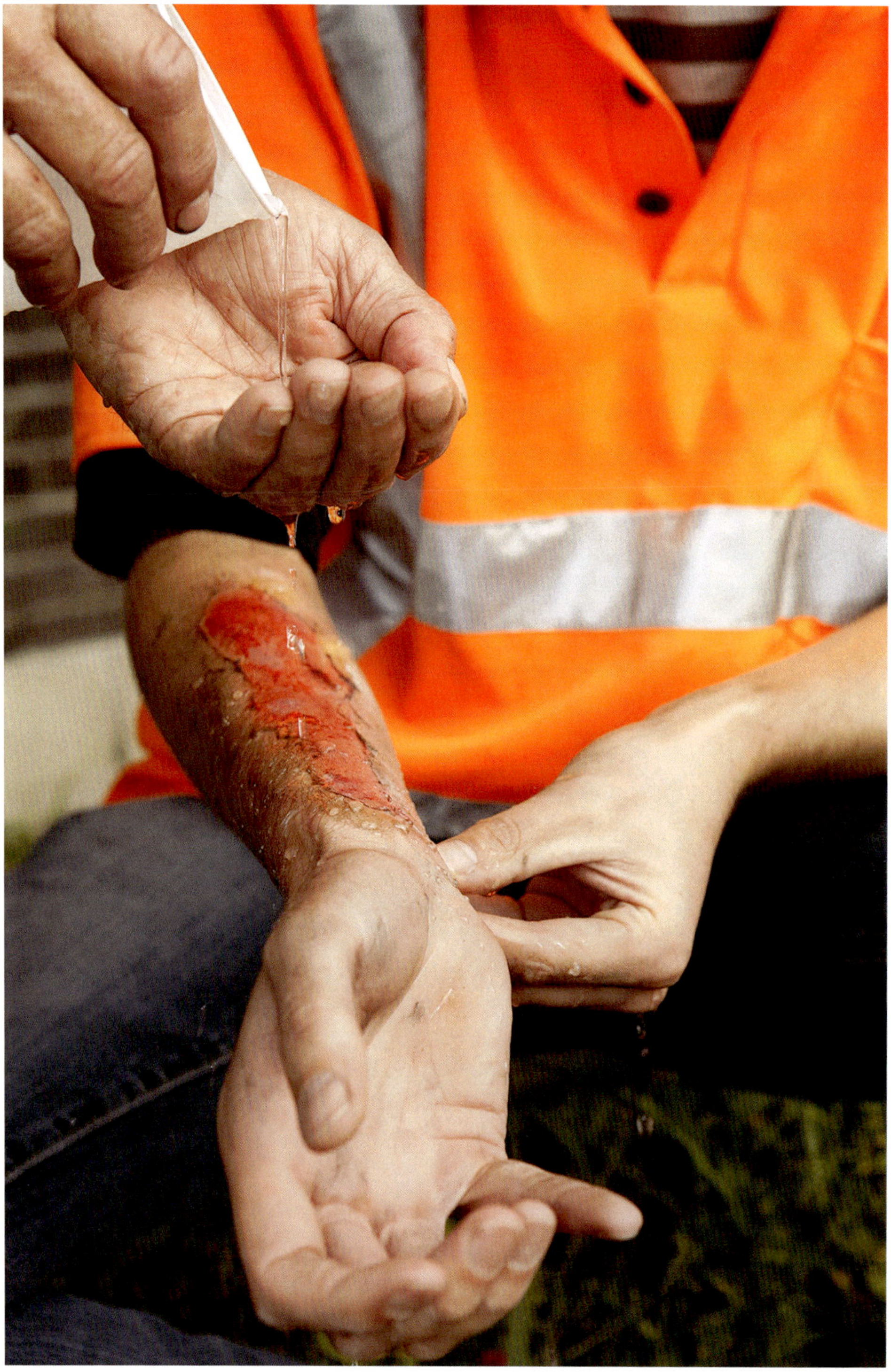

Credit: Shutterstock

CHAPTER 17
WOUNDS AND INJURIES

Wounds and injuries are great fun to do, either on their own or in combination with a character makeup. There are a lot of different kinds of wounds and a lot of different ways to do them. Let's jump in!

BROKEN NOSE

This is an example of creating the illusion of an injury with just highlight and shadow. For many of the makeups you've done so far, you've painted a shadow along the sides of the nose. You may have discovered already that, if the shadow isn't perfectly straight, your nose can look crooked. You're going to take advantage of that to simulate a broken nose.

Begin by applying a crooked highlight down the middle of your nose. Then add shadows to either side, following the shape you've created with the highlight. Once you blend the makeup you have an instant broken nose, which you can then dress with bruises, cuts or anything else.

PUTTY WOUNDS

You've already created large injuries using nose putty in the **Basic Zombie** makeup. The same technique can be used for small cuts, lacerations, bumps, swelling and other injuries. When the putty is in place, you can use a popsicle stick, small spatula or similar tool to sculpt the injury. Once you're happy with it, seal the putty with a couple layers of liquid latex, followed by makeup and blood.

As I mentioned with the Basic Zombie, nose putty works best on bony areas of the face without a lot of movement. Your forehead, nose, cheekbones and chin are ideal.

BRUISES

Bruises occur when there's bleeding underneath the skin, usually from a blunt object hitting the body. Bruises go through three main stages, each with their own color schemes, as the body first bleeds, then heals:

- Fresh – mostly reds and pinks as the bleeding starts.
- Aged – maroons, purples and blues begin to set in as the blood in the skin clots.
- Healing – the reds disappear, purples and blues become less pronounced, and greens,

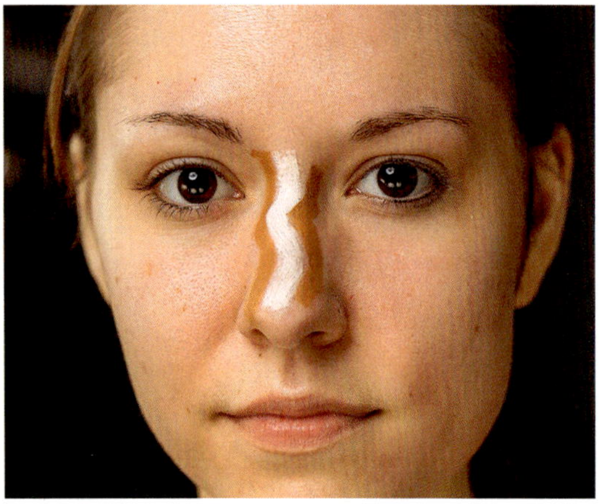

FIGURE 17.1 Broken nose before blending

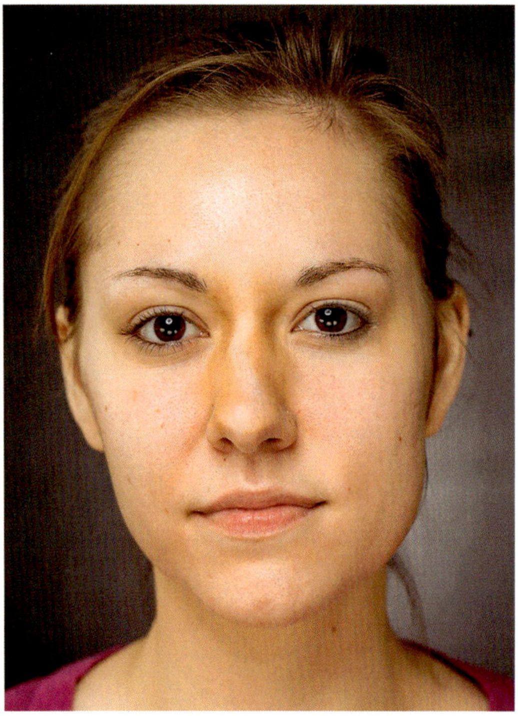

FIGURE 17.2 Broken nose after blending

yellows and browns become pronounced as the clotted blood is reabsorbed into the body.

Typically, you won't have to worry too much about the stage of a bruise for a makeup; a good generic one works just fine. Reference pictures are very useful when reproducing bruises, and you can find them all over the internet (seriously, just searching "black eye" will give you thousands of results).

Start by stippling some light red onto your skin with a brush, a makeup sponge or even with your fingers. This and all of the colors should be a little mottled; if you blend them too much, your bruise won't look realistic. I left an area bare in the middle of this bruise (Figure 17.3), which works like a highlight to make Ingrid's eye–cheek area look more swollen.

Once the red is in place, go in and add bits of maroon, blue and purple. Don't go overboard with these colors; keep it subtle! They can get out of control pretty easily.

When your bruise is done, give it a careful powdering to keep the colors from smearing together. Try experimenting with different combinations and intensities of colors to get different effects. For healing bruises, substitute the darker reds and maroons with greens and yellows.

SCRATCHES

Simple scratches are very easy to do: all you need is a coarse stipple sponge. Dip the sponge into red makeup and then lightly drag it across your skin. Use a light touch; if you're too heavy-handed, you'll just create a smear on your

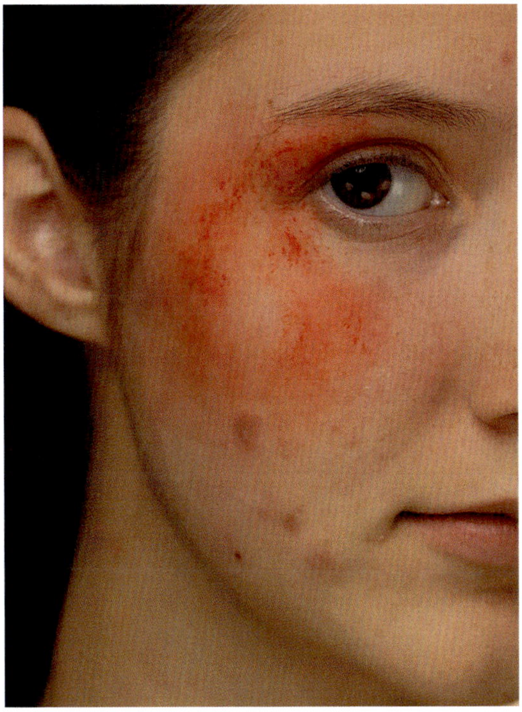

FIGURE 17.3 Starting a bruise with just red . . .

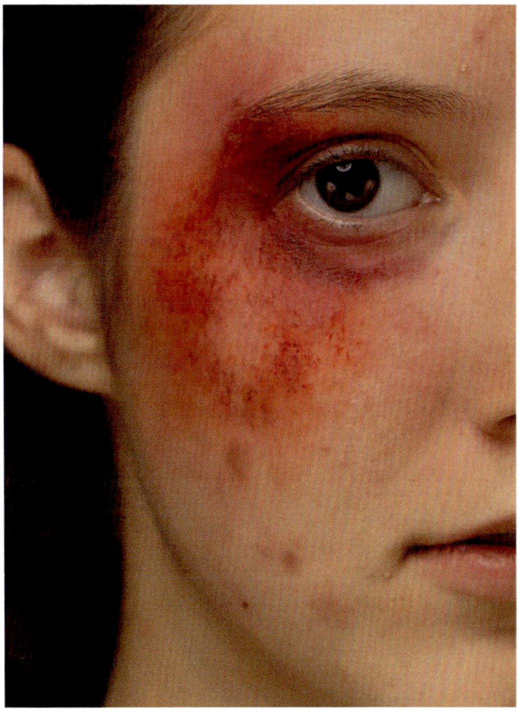

FIGURE 17.4 . . . Layering on darker colors

face. Once the scratches are in place, go back in and lightly stipple the heaviest areas to create more intensity. Finally, use the stipple sponge to dot on little spots of fake blood on top.

PAINTED-ON CUTS

Small, basic cuts can be done with just makeup, without using any kind of prosthetic.

Begin by applying a pinkish tone in the general area of the cut to simulate irritated skin. Use the edge of a makeup spatula to apply blood-colored makeup in a thin line in the center of the irritated area, creating a small cut. By varying how much makeup you apply as you drag the spatula across your skin, you can make the cut look more jagged and irregular.

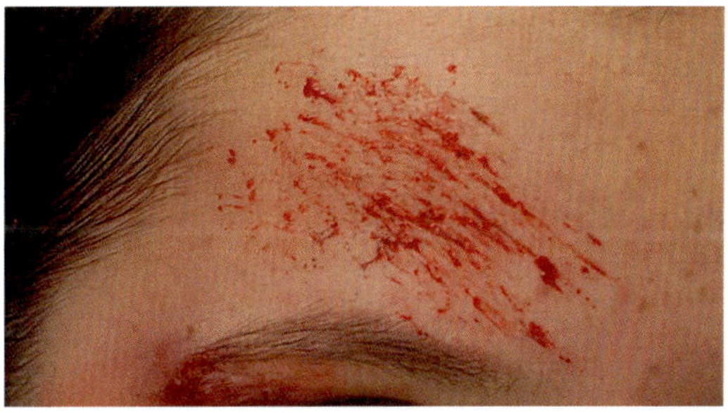

FIGURE 17.5 Scratches

Apply a bit of highlight around the edges of the cut to really make it pop and appear three-dimensional.

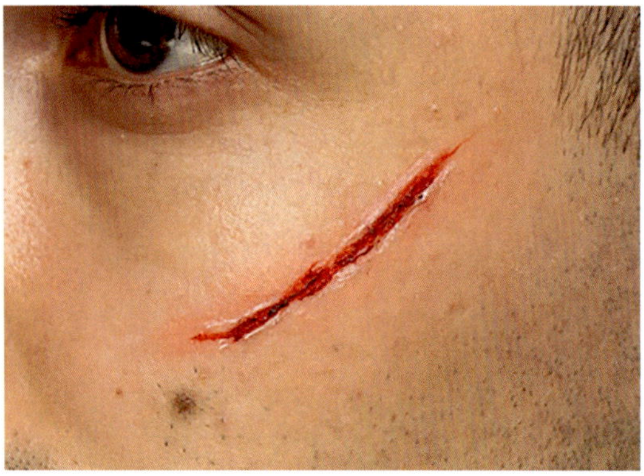

FIGURE 17.6 Painted-on cut

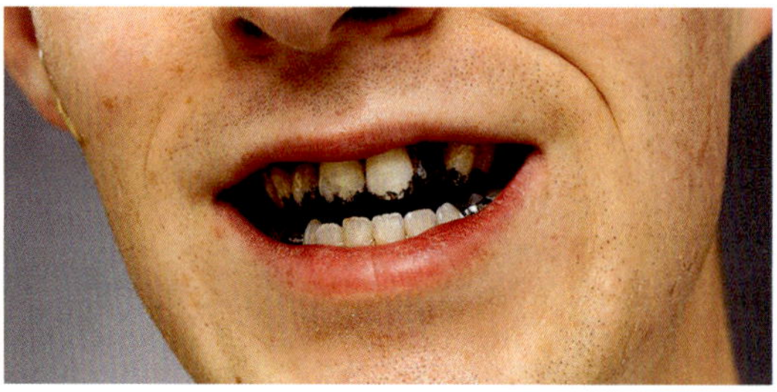

FIGURE 17.7 Broken and missing teeth

BROKEN TEETH

Using black tooth enamel, you can give the illusion of broken or missing teeth. Dry your teeth with a tissue before applying the enamel for the best results as it won't stick as well to wet teeth.

For a missing tooth, completely black it out with the enamel. Let it dry completely before you close your mouth again.

For broken teeth, paint the enamel irregularly to the edges of your teeth. When it dries, you'll have some mangled-looking choppers.

Tooth enamel comes in many others shades than just black, such as browns, yellows and greens. They're great for enhancing a character, but the enamel wears off after a while and will need to be reapplied if you're planning to wear your makeup for a long time (to get it off right away just brush your teeth as usual.)

RIGID COLLODION CUTS AND SCARS

Rigid collodion (also called non-flexible collodion) is a type of liquid plastic that you can paint directly onto your skin. As it dries, it puckers the skin, creating the illusion of a cut or scar. You can build up layers of collodion, intensifying the effect. A word of warning though: this stuff can be intense. Don't use collodion near your eyes. The fumes are pretty potent, and the plastic itself is not safe on your eyeballs. It can also be rough on your skin if you use it on the same spot over and over.

To create a cut or scar, first paint on some pinkish makeup for an old scar, or blood red for a cut (makeup pencils work well for this). On top of the drawn line, brush a layer of collodion onto your skin and let it dry. You can use a thin brush or stick to apply it, but make sure you clean any brush you use with rubbing alcohol right away so the collodion doesn't harden in the bristles.

You can create a smooth line for a cut caused by something sharp, or a more jagged line for a torn wound. Add extra layers of collodion to intensify the effect if needed.

You can also use rigid collodion for a larger scar, similar to burn tissue. To do this, stipple collodion randomly onto your skin in blotches and then let it dry. Repeat this process, randomly adding collodion a couple more times. The goal is to have some areas without much collodion (or none) and others with several layers. The result will be an irregular patch of scar tissue that looks pretty cool.

The downside to rigid collodion is that the edges peel up after a while. Several makeup

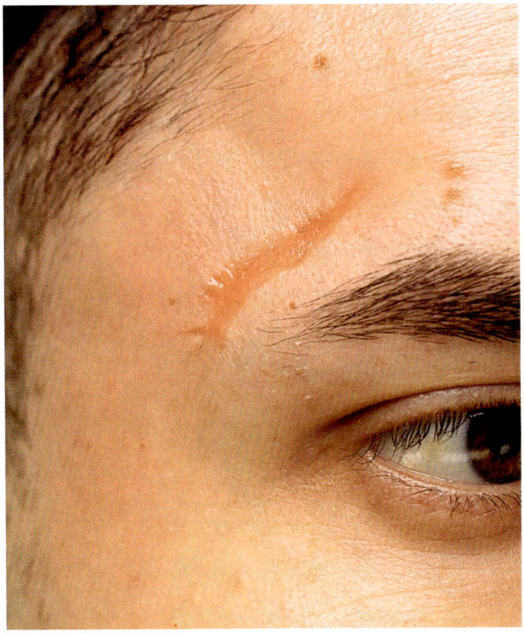

FIGURE 17.8 Rigid collodion scar

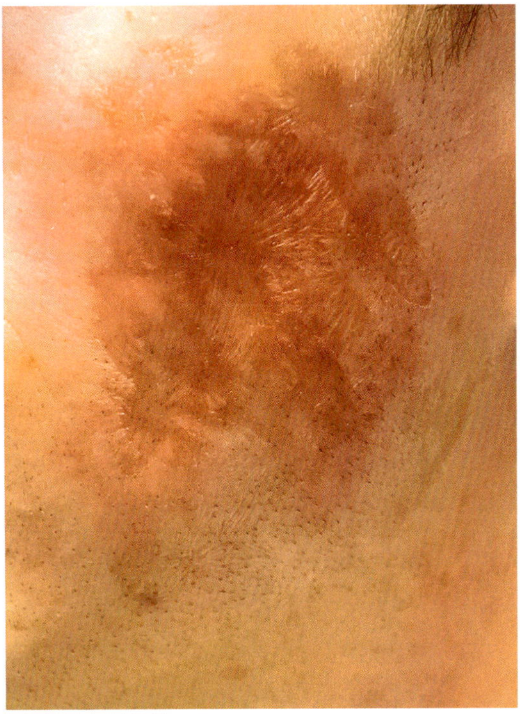

FIGURE 17.9 Larger collodion scar

companies make a product called flexible sealer. A layer of this on top of your wound will help it to stay in place.

When it's time to clean up, you can either peel the wound off or dissolve the collodion with a little acetone.

RAISED SCARS

Raised scars (called keloid scars in the medical world) can be created fairly easily using latex eyelash adhesive. Draw a bead of the adhesive along your skin and then let it dry (this can take a while; a hair dryer helps to speed things up). Make sure the latex is dry all the way through: if it's just skinned over but still wet underneath, it may tear open when you apply the makeup.

Once it's dry, paint it a pale pink if you have light skin. For dark skin, paint the scar a shade

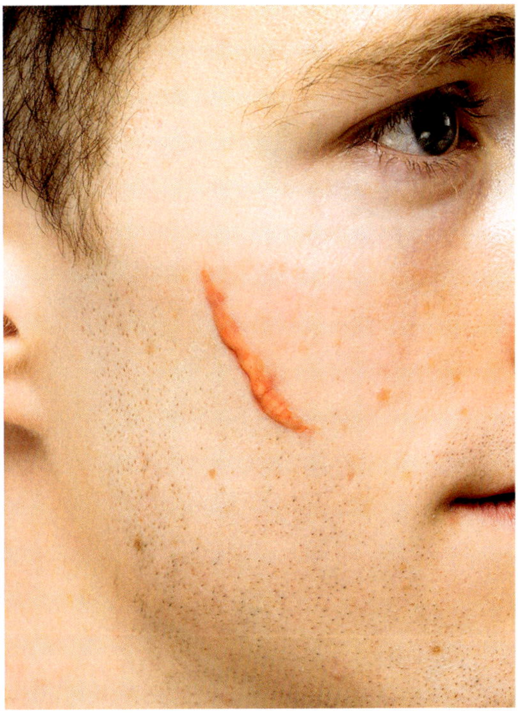

FIGURE 17.10 Raised scar using eyelash adhesive

or two darker than your natural skin tone. You can use this technique to create patterns found in ritual scarification and branding in addition to smaller scars.

LATEX AND TISSUE WOUNDS

Latex and tissue can be used to create irregular, gaping wounds fairly easily. The procedure is similar to the open sores you've done a few times already. Apply a single layer of latex and tissue to your skin, sealing it with a top coat of latex. You want this to be as smooth as possible to blend into your skin (unless you're already using latex and tissue to create skin texture).

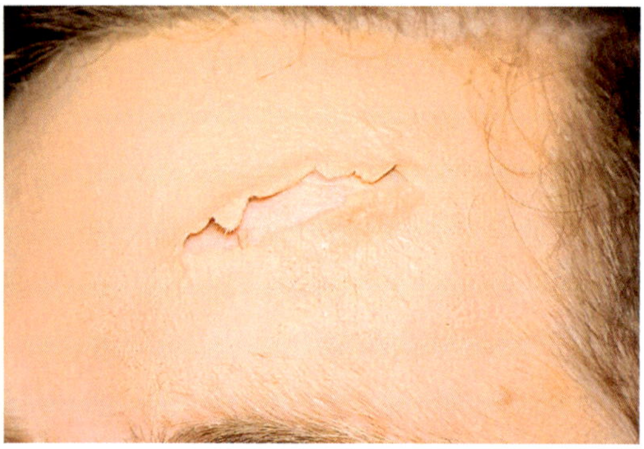

FIGURE 17.11 Latex and tissue wound (before color)

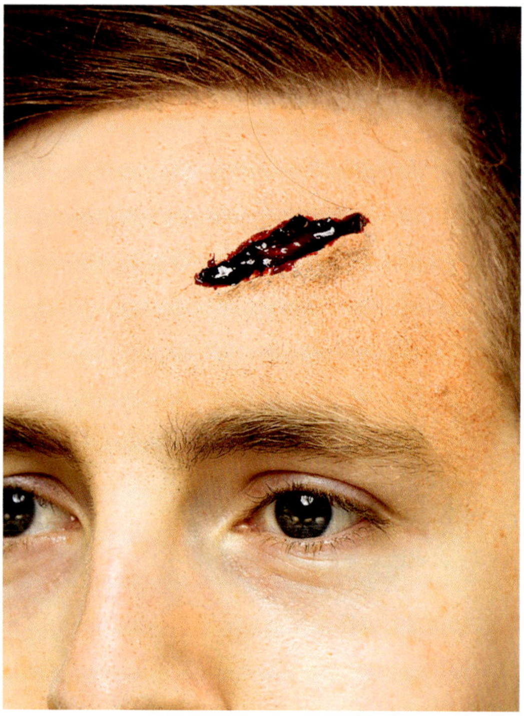

FIGURE 17.12 Finished latex and tissue wound

Once everything is dry, powder the latex and use tweezers to tear the center of the latex open, forming a cut. Unlike the sores, powdering first keeps the latex from rolling back and sticking to itself. Instead, it will look like ragged flaps of skin around the wound. Finish the effect with makeup and blood.

CHAPTER 18
HAIR AND STUBBLE

Laying hair directly onto the skin is a technique that has been used in movies and theater for many, many years. The technique isn't too complicated, but it definitely takes some practice to make it look real.

The sort of hair you're going to use is called **crepe hair** or **crepe wool.** Both terms refer to the same thing: a tight braid of wool that is sold in many colors in costume shops. The wool isn't the best quality in the world, but it works well for adding hair to makeups. Before you can use it, however, you will need to do some prep work.

PREPARING CREPE WOOL

Begin by removing the wool from the two strings it's braided onto. You can do this by carefully cutting the strings and pulling them out of the braid. Already the wool will begin to relax, but it will still be pretty kinky and difficult to work with. The next step is to straighten the wool.

Heat some water in a pot to near-boiling and then drop a section of wool into it. *Immediately* fish the wool out with a stick or spoon. Those few seconds in the hot water will cause the wool to completely relax. You'll find that the wool is now three or four times longer than it was when it was braided! It goes a long way.

FIGURE 18.1 Crepe wool as packaged (top), straightened (middle), fluffed and ready to use (bottom)

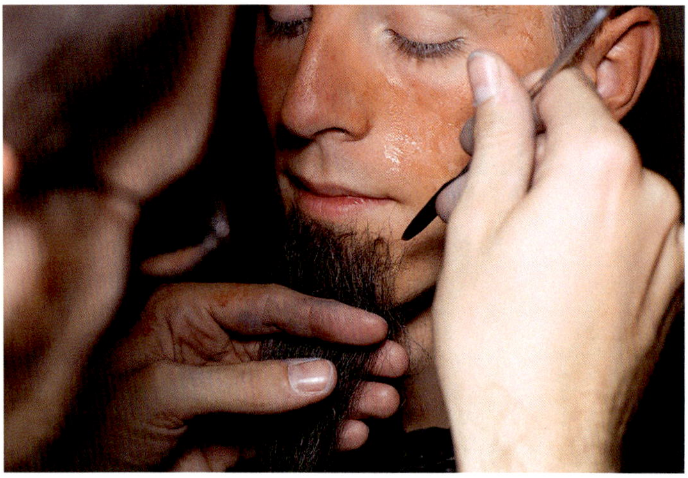

FIGURE 18.2 Laying crepe wool into adhesive

Hang the wet wool up to dry overnight. Once it's dry, you can pull it apart into fluffy bunches that are easier to work with.

If you own a handheld garment steamer (used to get wrinkles out of clothes), you can straighten crepe wool without the wait time. After you remove the strings, use the hot steam to loosen the curl until it has the level of waviness you want. This technique gives you a lot more control, but, of course, you need to own a steamer.

To blend multiple colors of crepe wool, hold a few different bunches together by their ends and pull them apart. Then put them together again and repeat the process. Every time you pull the wool apart, the colors will mix a little more. This technique is useful for creating salt-and-pepper effects, plus, mixing a few different shades together always looks more realistic than a single color.

I usually roll each color of prepped wool in a paper towel and then keep all of the rolls stored in a large freezer bag. It helps to keep everything organized without getting hair everywhere.

LAYING HAIR

To lay the hair onto your skin, pull a small amount from the bundle and cut the end straight with a sharp pair of scissors. It's not a bad idea to lay out several of these small amounts in advance; that way, you don't have to stop and start constantly as you're laying the hair.

There are several adhesives you can use for this process, but the two that are easiest to get are spirit gum and liquid latex. Brush a small amount of either onto your skin. Let spirit gum get tacky; work with latex while it's still wet. Place the cut ends of the hair into the adhesive and hold them in place until they stick. You can use the flat side of a brush handle or craft stick to press the hair more firmly against your skin, but make sure the hair is standing up in the adhesive rather than smashed flat (which does not look like it's growing naturally out of the skin).

Continue adding small amounts of hair to your skin until the area you're working on is covered. Pay attention to the direction the hair would naturally grow! For beards, you typically want to start under your chin and work your way up; for mustaches and eyebrows, start from the outer edges and work your way in. On a bald head, you'd start at the back of the neck and then work your way up and around to the forehead. This approach means the second layer of hair will lay nicely on top of the first, then the third layer on top of the second, and so on. There's a chart for you to work off at the end of this chapter.

Most of this hair you can "chunk in," but when you get close to the outer edges you want to be more delicate. Add small, thin amounts of hair at a time so that it creates a natural hairline where you can see a bit of your skin through the hair (look at your own hairline to see what I mean).

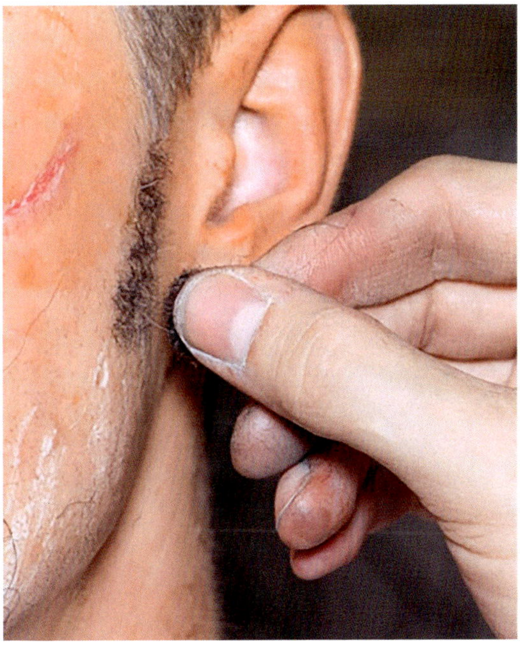

FIGURE 18.3 Applying a ball of crepe wool stubble to adhesive

The laid hair will be pretty bushy, so lightly go through it with a wide-toothed comb to remove excess. You can then trim the finished hair however you want. When it's time for removal, use rubbing alcohol for spirit gum or just peel the latex off. That's one advantage to using latex – if you're careful, you can reuse the beard! You can even build up a latex beard on a plastic face form (you can often find them in art supply stores) instead of working directly on your face.

Author's Note: *When writing this book, one of my main goals was that you would be able to find all of your materials locally and inexpensively. This is one time that I'm going to cheat. You can purchase an adhesive called Pros-Aide online (and in some makeup stores if you live in a bigger city) that is far superior for laying crepe wool. It stays sticky after it dries, so that you can work without having wet adhesive getting all over everything. Just brush some on, let it dry and press cut ends of the wool in place. Easy peasy. If you buy some, you can also use it in place of spirit gum for just about every makeup in this book. Be aware that you will also need to buy Pros-Aide Remover or isopropyl myristate to remove it from your skin.*

LAYING STUBBLE

Laying chopped hair stubble is a much more realistic way to create an unshaved character than using a stipple sponge. Begin by chopping some crepe wool into tiny pieces with a sharp pair of scissors. You want bits that are ⅛–¼-inch long. Collect these trimmings in a bowl as you work, otherwise they will get everywhere. You can use an electric trimmer instead of scissors if you want: it makes the work go much more quickly.

Brush some adhesive onto your skin and then use a fluffy makeup brush to gather up some chopped hair. Gently brush the hair onto the tacky adhesive, using a light touch and brushing in the direction the stubble would naturally grow. Continue adding more stubble until the entire area is filled. Use a fine-toothed comb or mascara wand to brush the stubble, aligning the hairs as best as you can and breaking up any clumps.

Another technique is to gather some of these trimmings into a ball. Rolling that ball between your fingers will help it to keep it from falling apart. After applying the adhesive to your skin, lightly tap the ball onto it. The adhesive will grab some of the hairs, leaving a patch of realistic stubble. Keep working in small sections until you have filled in the entire area you're working on.

Once again, it's important to keep a very light touch when applying chopped hair stubble. If you press too hard, you'll end up with a big hairy blob that's pretty hard to fix without having to start over. Take your time: patience and finesse are your friends when laying hair.

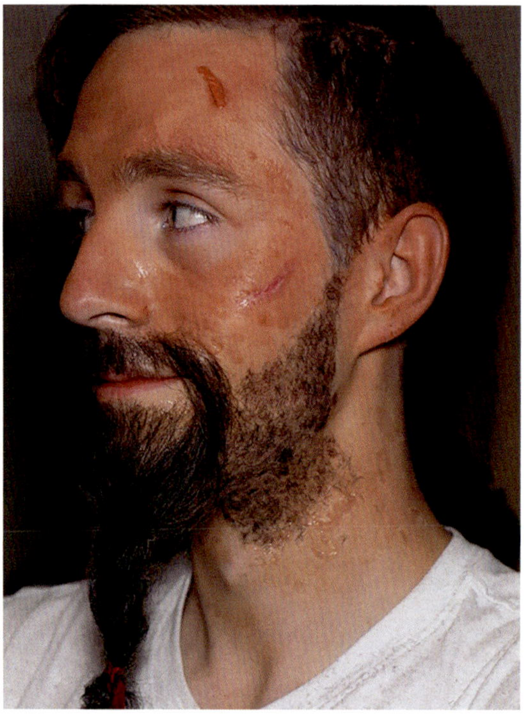

FIGURE 18.4 **Combining a hand-laid goatee with chopped hair stubble**

A third method is to lightly press some heavy mesh or netting from a fabric store into the adhesive. Apply the stubble, then peel the mesh off in the direction of the hair growth. The mesh will automatically align the hairs stuck to your face. This technique lets you work on larger areas at once, but you also have to work quickly so the adhesive doesn't dry and stick the mesh to your skin.

Eyebrows
Layer from the outside in

Mustache
Layer from the outside in

Credit: Christopher Payne

Credit: Christopher Payne

CHAPTER 19

MAKING BASIC PROSTHETICS

You were introduced to prosthetics with the **Witch** makeup, though technically the rivets on the **Robot** and the boils on the **Plague** victim count as prosthetics as well. In its broadest definition, a prosthetic is anything that is glued to your face (not counting things such as crepe wool and false eyelashes).

Costume shops often sell the simple sorts of rubber noses and chins that you used on the Witch, and some are starting to carry more advanced foam latex prosthetics. The process for making these prosthetics is fairly complicated and involves sculpting the prosthetic in clay, making a mold of it and producing final pieces out of that mold. The more complicated the prosthetic, the more complicated the process.

There is an easier technique that you can use to make basic rubber prosthetics yourself. Simple noses, ears, horns and other items can be made in this way.

First, sculpt the rough shape that you want in paper clay, which dries in a day or two when exposed to the air. Paper clay is available in any craft store. While sculpting, you can spray the clay with water to make it more workable. Overexaggerate your forms and shapes a little bit – you'll lose some detail in the next step, so you want to compensate for that in your sculpture. For this ear, my only sculpting tools were my fingers and a popsicle stick. If you want, you can use a plastic mask or other face form as a base when sculpting noses, chins, etc.

Once your sculpture is dry, brush on 10–12 layers of liquid latex, front and back (if there is a back). Dry each layer before adding the next and try to keep your edges only a couple of layers thick so that they will be easier to blend into your skin. If you're working on a face form, you don't have to wait for the clay to dry because it's supported – just use a light touch as you stipple the latex.

When all the latex is in place, powder it and peel it off the clay form, powdering the inside as you go. You now have a simple, custom prosthetic!

The ears I've made on the next page will make an appearance later in the book.

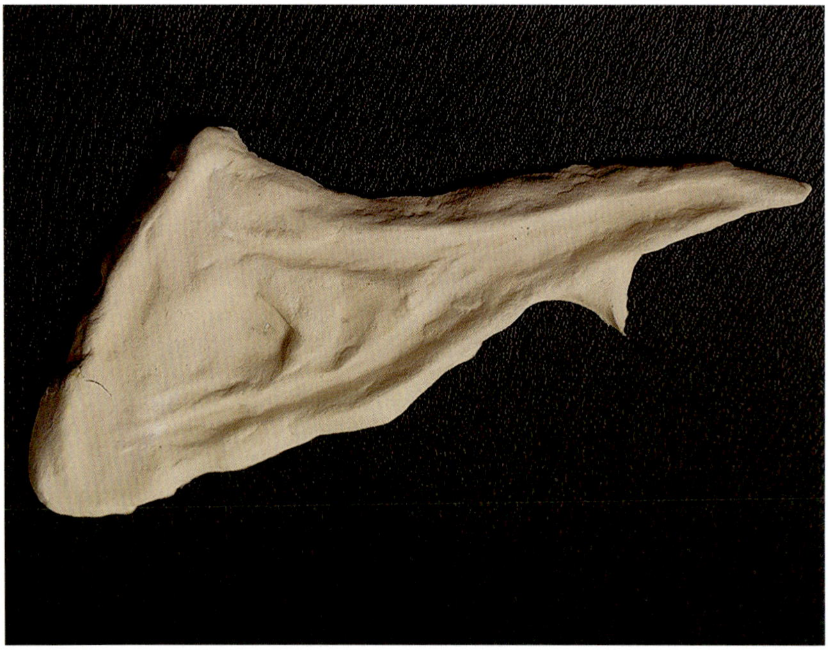

FIGURE 19.1 A pointed monster ear sculpted in paper clay

FIGURE 19.2 The latex version

Credit: Christopher Payne

CHAPTER 20

CHARACTER DESIGN

If you're anything like me, a lot of the time you'll want to just break out the makeup and start creating a monster on the spot. However, there are many times when doing a bit of character design in advance is helpful. It saves time and materials having an idea of what you want to do in advance.

There are several ways of designing a character, ranging from a simple pencil sketch to full-on Photoshop designs. Figure 20.1 is an example of the sort of design work you see done for movies, created by concept artist Jerad Marantz. Jerad has done creature and character design for some of Hollywood's biggest blockbusters in recent years.

This is far more elaborate than you will need for most purposes outside the film industry. There's a much easier way that you can create a makeup design right on a person's picture.

Begin with a photo of your subject. It's usually best to use a three-quarter perspective; that way you can plan out the front and side of the face at the same time. Some characters (such as the **Robot**) may be easier to design with straight-on pictures of the front and side.

FIGURE 20.1 **A digital creature design. (Image reproduced by permission of Jerad S. Marantz)**

Credit: Jerad S. Marantz

Print out the picture as large as can fit on a sheet of paper. If you have access to Photoshop or a similar program, it's helpful to reduce the opacity so the picture is more ghostly (50% is usually good).

Once you have the print in front of you, start sketching right on top of it using pastel chalks. These chalks come in stick form (good for foundation, highlight and shadow and large areas) and pencil form (good for adding detail as you can sharpen them to a fine point). You can blend the colors together right on the paper using your fingers or paper blending tools called tortillons.

Begin with the basic foundation, highlight and shadow understructure before you layer on wrinkles, wounds or other details. As with makeup, it will be very hard to add this understructure later if there are already details in the way. Shape the face first and then dress it up. So long as you don't go too heavy, you'll still be able to see your face through the chalk, making the whole process *much* easier than drawing a whole face from scratch. When you're done, giving your rendering a light coating of a spray fixative from any art store (or even hairspray) will protect it.

I've never been very good at drawing, so this technique has helped me design characters for many plays and movies. With a little practice, it's a great low-tech method of working out the details for a makeup before you break out the glue and blood.

In Figures 20.2–20.5, you'll find four designs that I sketched up, using my own face as a starting point.

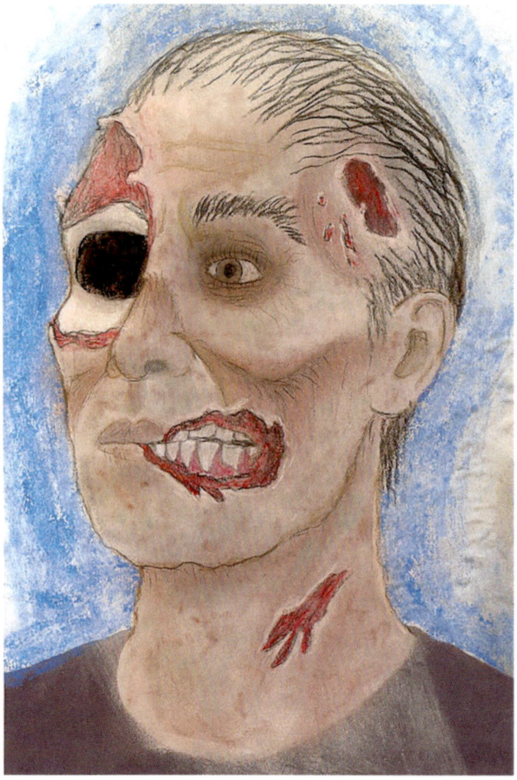

FIGURE 20.2

Credit: Christopher Payne

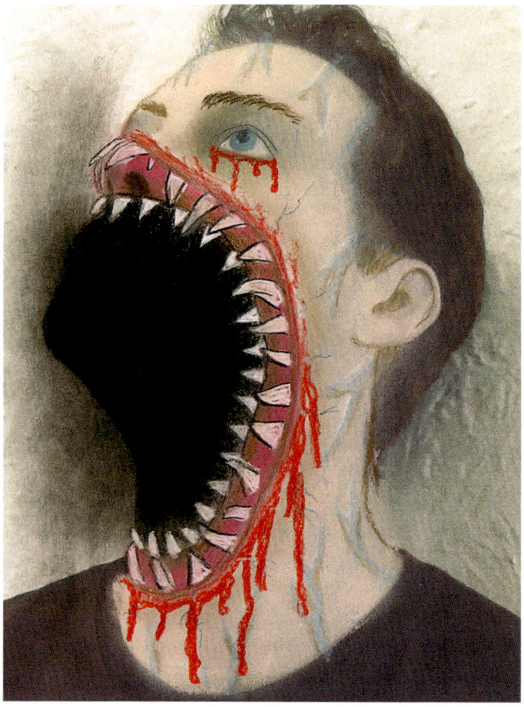

FIGURE 20.3

Credit: Christopher Payne

FIGURE 20.4

Credit: Christopher Payne

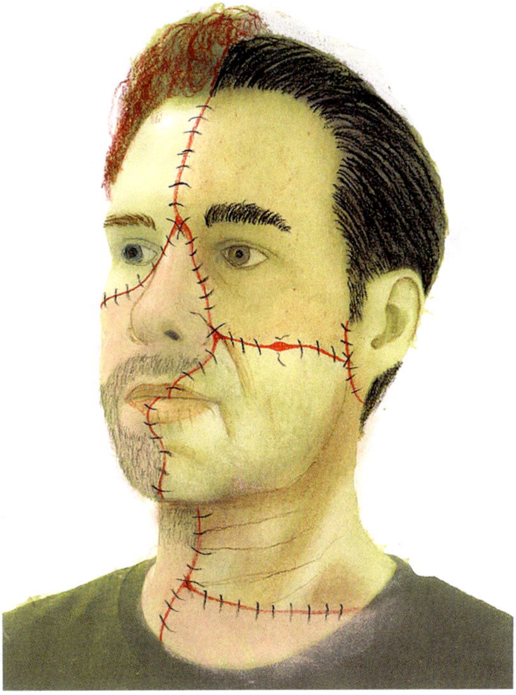

FIGURE 20.5

Credit: Christopher Payne

SECTION 3

ADVANCED MAKEUP

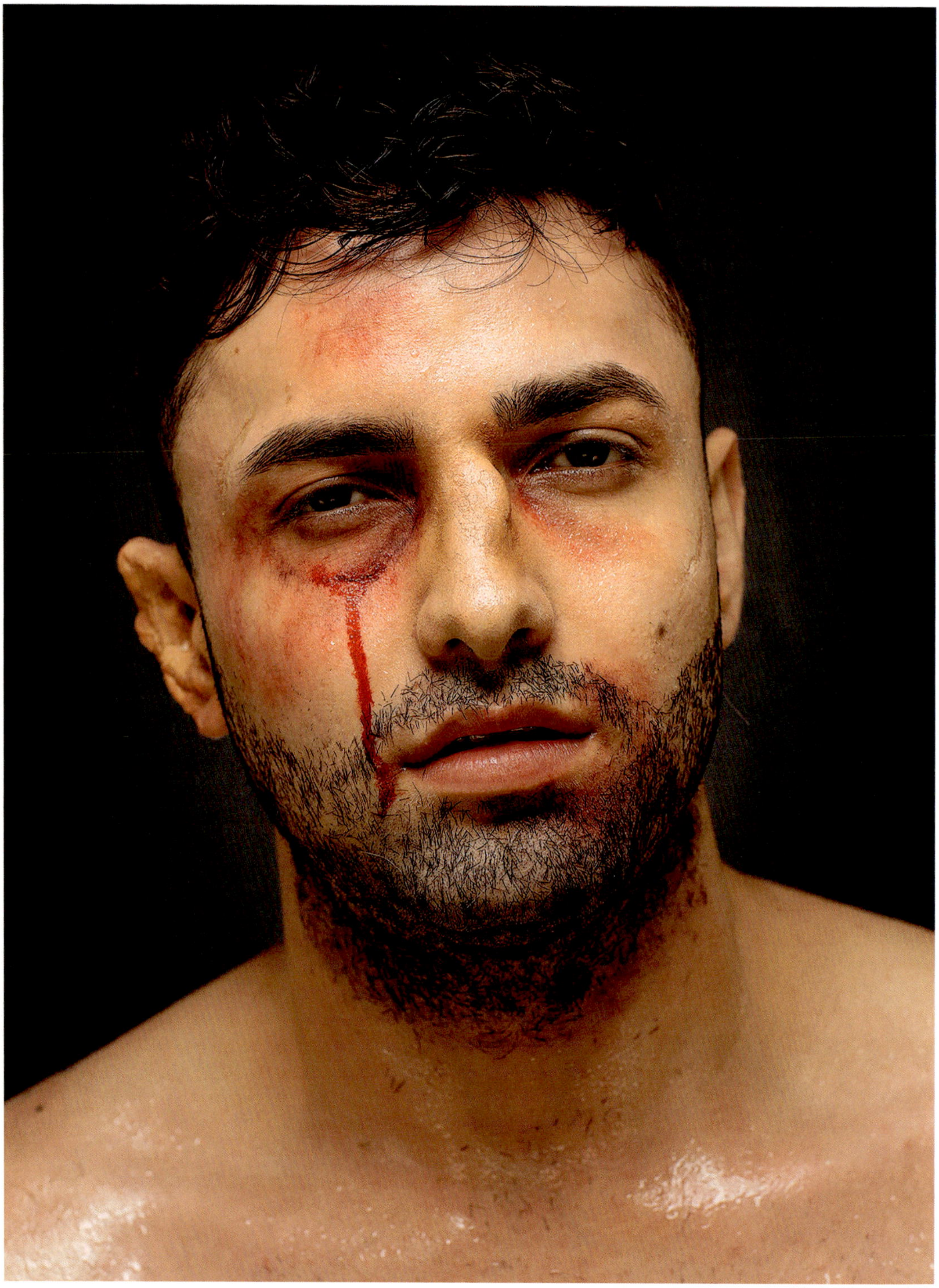

CHAPTER 21
THE CHAMP

For the first makeup in the advanced section, let's put together a lot of the injury and texture techniques you've learned. **The Champ** will be a boxer who's just lost a fight, and probably quite a few before that. As fighters go, this guy's a real bum.

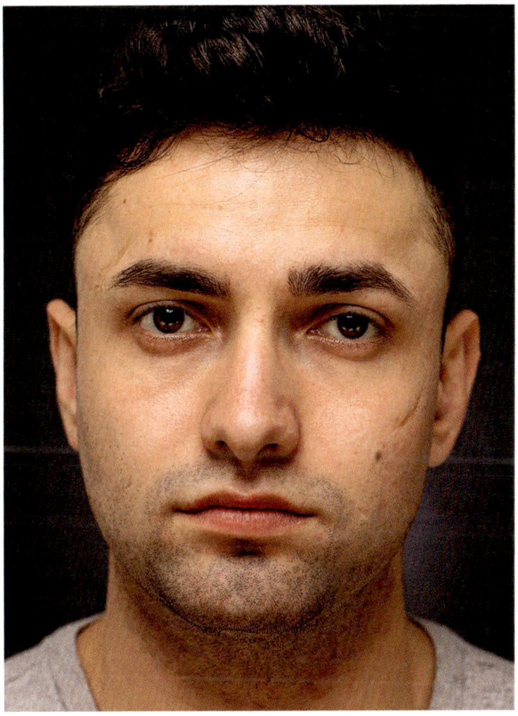

FIGURE 21.1 Step 1

STEP 1

Begin by adding a few old scars using rigid collodion. You can add as many as you want, but if you go crazy you may end up with a sci-fi soldier sort of character.

STEP 2

Add a broken nose with a lump of putty on one side of your nose. Play with the shape until it looks natural and seal it with liquid latex when it's good.

STEP 3

Apply foundation to your face and neck, working carefully on the wax so it doesn't distort. Use castor oil to make a little RMG for the latex on your nose. You can use some of the highlight and shadow techniques from the painted-on broken nose in the **Wounds and Injuries** chapter to make the nose look even more crooked.

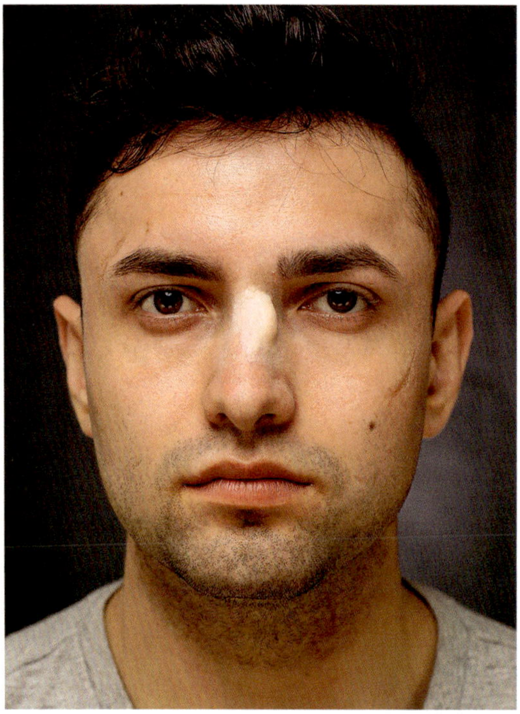

FIGURE 21.2 Step 2

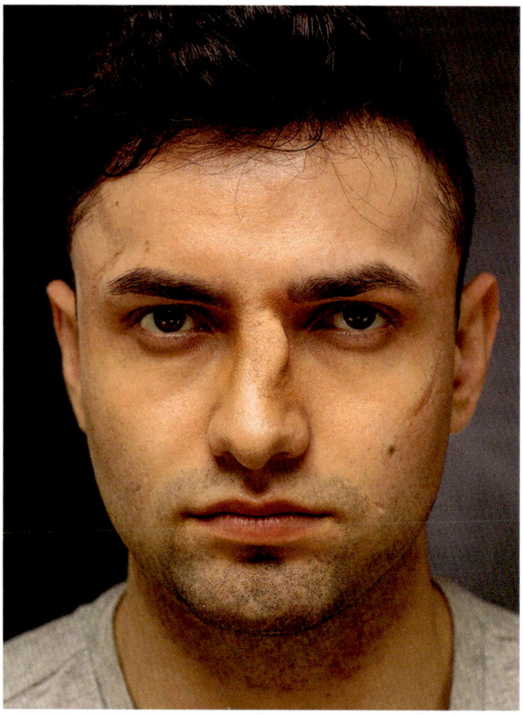

FIGURE 21.3 Step 3

STEP 4

Use cotton and latex to give yourself a cauliflower ear, a common injury for boxers. I used small tufts of cotton, adding a bit at a time to the latex until I had a shape I liked.

Seal the ear with a layer of latex and tissue for smoother skin if you want.

STEP 5

Add some nice fresh bruises to your boxer by stippling on reds and maroons. Like in the **Wounds and Injuries** chapter, I left bare spots on Misael's cheek and next to his mouth to make those areas seem swollen. You can also stuff a couple of cotton balls into your mouth between your cheek and teeth to create a 3D swelling effect.

STEP 6

Add a fresh cut or two, either with more collodion or just using makeup (I did the latter; because the cut is right under his eye, the fumes from collodion would have been irritating).

By now, the latex on your ear should be completely dry, so add foundation. Have a look at your other ear and match any redness you may have; the ears are often redder than the rest of your face because a bit of light passes through them.

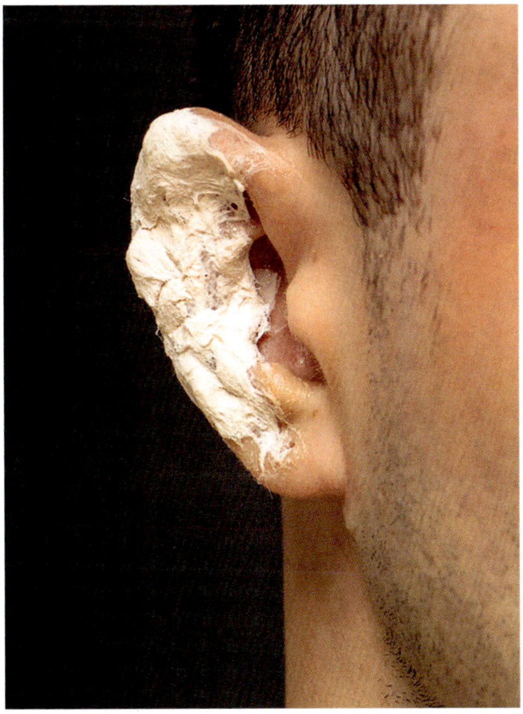

FIGURE 21.4 Step 4

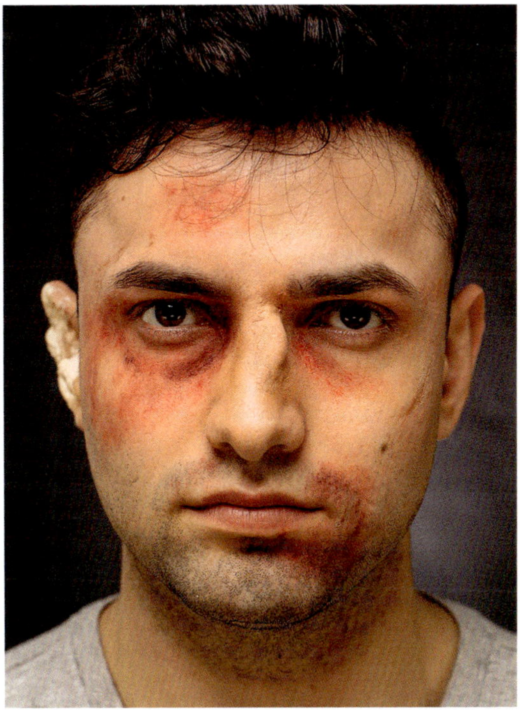

FIGURE 21.5 Step 5

STEP 7

Even though Misael already had light stubble on the day we did this makeup, I decided to add some chopped hair scruff on his face and neck. The idea is that this boxer is such a loser he didn't even bother to clean himself up before the fight.

For this stubble, I used the first technique described in the **Hair and Stubble** chapter, carefully brushing the chopped hair into the glue and then using a disposable mascara wand to align everything in the proper direction.

STEP 8

Finish the makeup with a bit of fresh blood dripping from any cuts. If your boxer is just leaving the fight, you can spray on some water and glycerin to make him look sweaty.

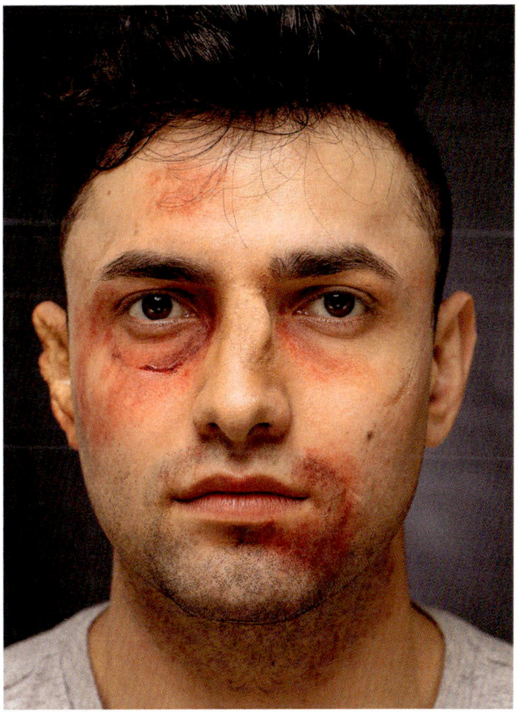

FIGURE 21.6 Step 6

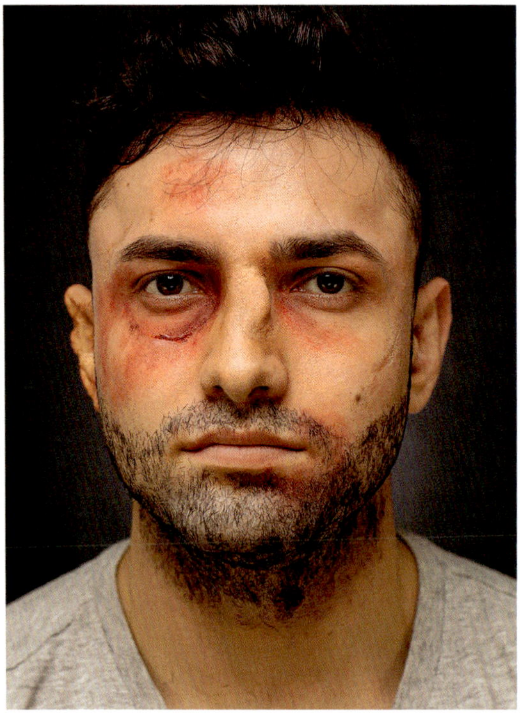

FIGURE 21.7 Step 7

FIGURE 21.8 Adding sweat

As I mentioned in this book's introduction, one of my heroes in the world of makeup is a man named Dick Smith. I got to meet him a few times before he passed away, and I'll never forget the story he told me of working on the 1962 boxing film *Requiem for a Heavyweight*.

Legendary boxer Muhammad Ali (then known as Cassius Clay) appears at the beginning of the film, and it was Smith's job to keep him looking sweaty throughout the long filming day. Apparently, Ali *hated* the water and glycerin mix that Smith was using for sweat and would go out of his way to avoid being sprayed down. He would even try to duck out of the way when Smith approached him in the ring, forcing the beleaguered makeup artist to go running after him.

Dick told me this story the first time I met him and said with a laugh that he's the only person to have ever chased Muhammad Ali around the ring with a spray bottle and lived to tell the tale.

CHAPTER 22

GRIM REAPER

A skull makeup is great on Halloween, because it works for many different characters. You can use it for a **Grim Reaper**, incorporate it into a zombie makeup, or use it for an original creation. This makeup will use many of the highlight and shadow techniques previously learned, creating both hard and soft edges in the same character. Research using pictures of real skulls can be really useful when creating this character. I had a lot of skull pictures in front of me as I did Dan's makeup.

Before you start, you'll want to explore your face with your fingers, feeling the skull beneath. You need a good understanding of where your eye sockets, cheekbones, teeth and other features lie so the makeup fits your face.

STEP 1

Apply a bald cap, following the procedure described in the **Bald Caps** chapter. Don't cut out the ears from your cap; you want to keep them covered to give the illusion of a smooth skull.

If you're planning to wear a hood to cover your hair, you can skip the bald cap and go straight to the next step. Slick your hair back with some gel to make sure it doesn't fall into your face.

STEP 2

Block out your eyebrows following the steps outlined in the **Blocking Out Hair** chapter.

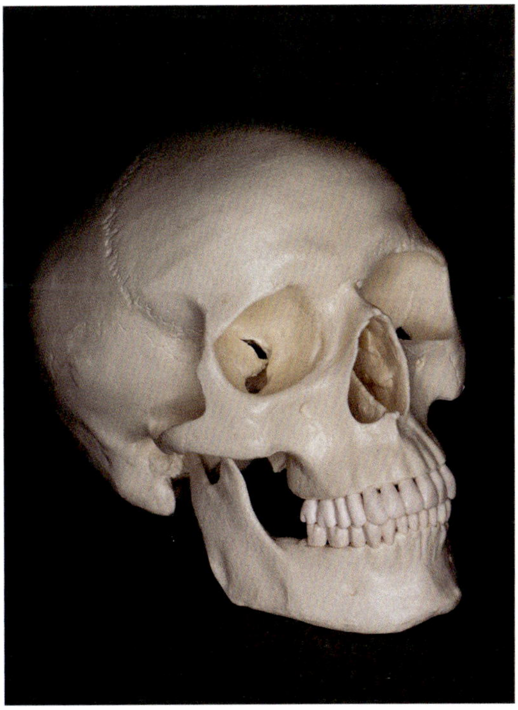

FIGURE 22.1

Credit: Christopher Payne

STEP 3

Draw the locations of the eye sockets, nose, jaw and other major structures of the skull with a makeup pencil. This is easiest to do on your clean skin because you can poke and prod without disturbing the foundation.

I'm going to cheat a little on the nose, anatomically speaking. Because I can't actually remove it, I'll have to incorporate its shape into the makeup.

STEP 4

Apply a foundation of ivory or white RMG makeup on the bald cap and a matching cream makeup to the other areas of your head and neck that will be bone. Ivory is a more realistic skull color, but you can use white if you want your makeup to stand out more. Skip the eye sockets,

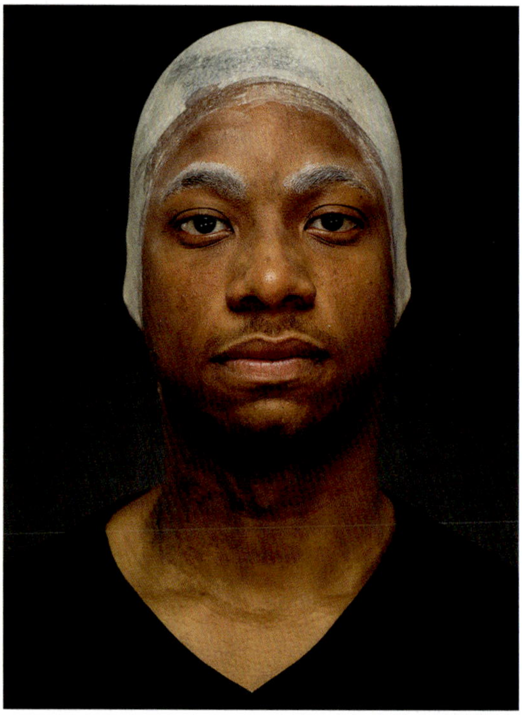

FIGURE 22.2 Steps 1 and 2

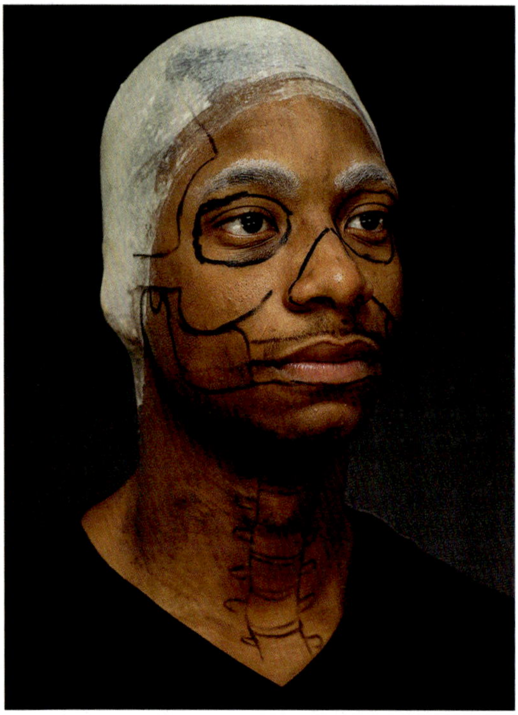

FIGURE 22.3 Step 3

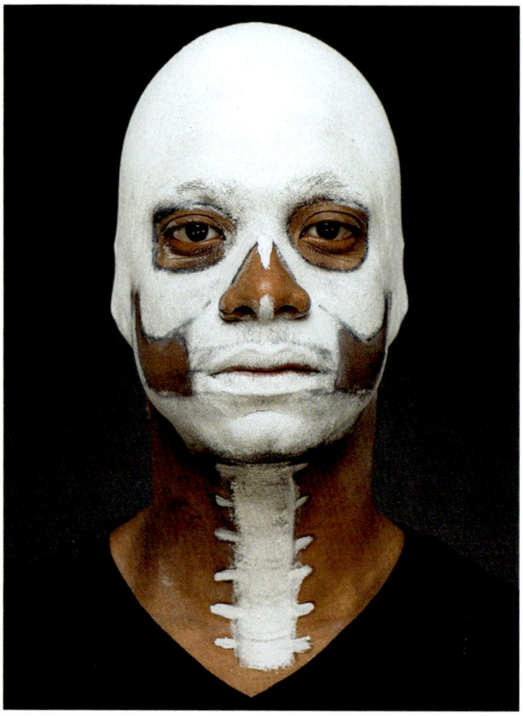

FIGURE 22.4 Step 4

nose and other areas you know you'll be filling in with black. If you try to do black over a heavy white foundation, it will just go gray.

STEP 5

Heavily powder the makeup to set it, using neutral powder or even baby powder as the makeup is so light.

STEP 6

Fill in the eye sockets, nose and other exposed areas with black makeup, following your skull photos as a guide. You'll notice that I left most of the neck clean until the very end; this was just to avoid any possible smearing as Dan turned his head.

STEP 7

Begin shadowing the temples using either brown (on an ivory foundation) or gray (on white), first drawing a hard line at the forward edge and then fading the color back. Fading out the makeup as it goes back creates the illusion of a hard edge in the front, and a fading soft edge as the skull fills out again above the ears.

Use the same technique to add other shadows to your face, using pictures of a real skull as a guide.

Author's Note: *Notice how I added some white to the black area underneath the cheekbone, fading it out as it goes back. This will help to make the teeth look like they go back into the skull rather than just being painted onto the cheeks.*

FIGURE 22.5 Step 6

FIGURE 22.6 Step 7

STEP 8

Draw on the teeth, extending out onto your cheeks. Add shadows on the lip–chin area between each tooth to simulate the natural dips on the jawbones. You can try this with a black makeup pencil, but I found it was easier using cream makeup and a fine brush.

STEP 9

Give everything a final, careful powdering to set the makeup.

As it turns out, the robe I used for the final picture hid enough of Dan's head that I could have easily skipped the bald cap. C'est la vie!

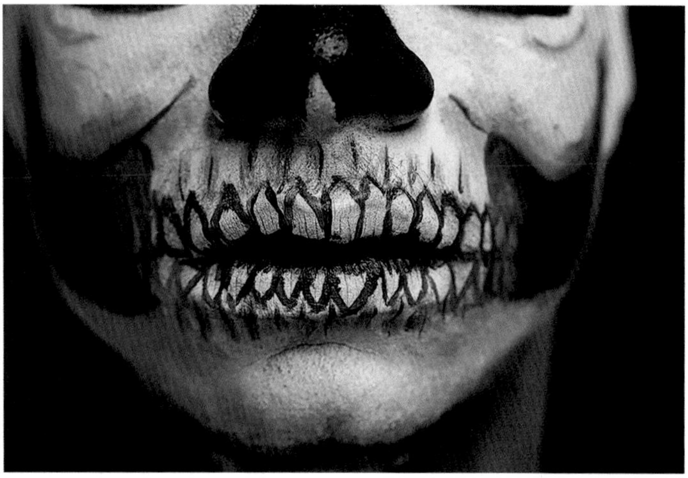

FIGURE 22.7 Step 8

CHAPTER 23
GIGGLES

Coulrophobia is the scientific term for a pretty common phobia: the fear of clowns. Some people couldn't care less about all the ghouls and goblins in the world, but bring a clown into the room and they'll go running for the hills.

Giggles is going to take the concept of a scary clown and push it a step further by making it look like you have a creepy grin carved right into your face, with the eyes ripped out for good measure. It's a buildup version of a prosthetic makeup I've done a few times for Halloween, and it always gets a great reaction.

You're going to begin by premaking some teeth prosthetics, but you can build the teeth up directly on your face if you prefer. Doing them in advance saves you some time in the makeup chair.

STEP 1

Cut white fake fingernails (the kind you find in the cosmetics section of a drugstore) into teeth shapes. Look at your own teeth as you work to get the sizes and shapes right.

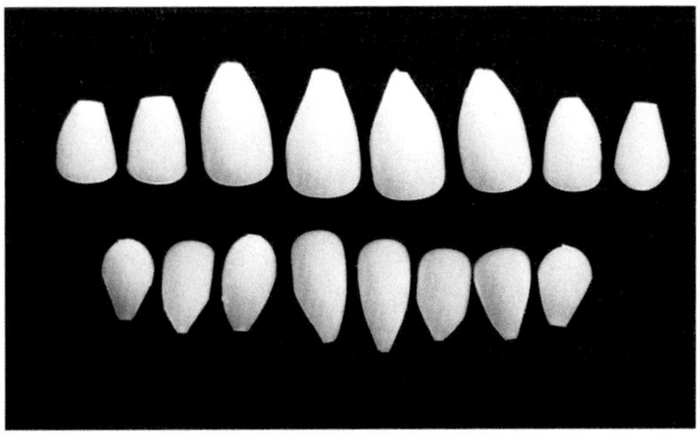

FIGURE 23.1 Step 1

Credit: Christopher Payne

STEP 2

Glue a small strip of nylon or tulle (a mesh sold at fabric stores) to the back of each tooth with super glue, extending a ¼-inch above the top of the tooth (see this in the Step 3 photo, Figure 23.2). The purpose of the tulle is to give the latex you're about to use something to grab onto. Without it, the smooth teeth could come loose pretty easily.

STEP 3

Add a drop of red food coloring to some liquid latex to tint it pink and then apply a layer of cotton and latex to the upper lip of a generic plastic mask or similar face form. Because this will be thin, you can actually soak the cotton in the latex. Squeegee most of the latex back out with your fingers before you put it on the mask.

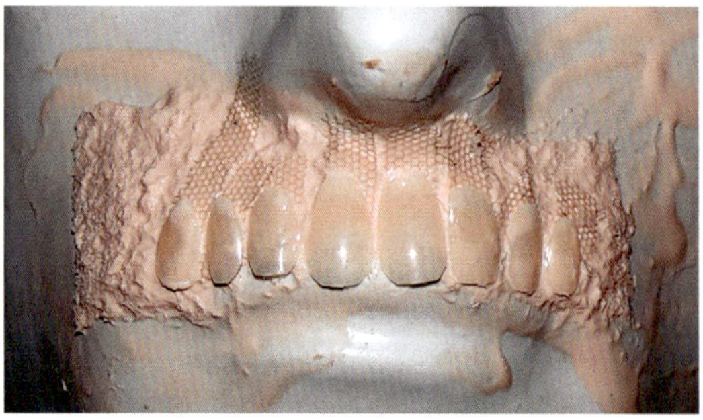

FIGURE 23.2 Step 3

Credit: Christopher Payne

STEP 4

While the latex is wet, press the upper teeth you made earlier into it. Then apply more cotton and latex on top to form the gums (this is similar to the technique in the **Teeth** chapter, just with different materials). Use a toothpick or similar small stick to sculpt the shape you want into the wet cotton.

Let this prosthetic dry, then powder it and slowly peel if off of the mask (powder underneath it as you peel).

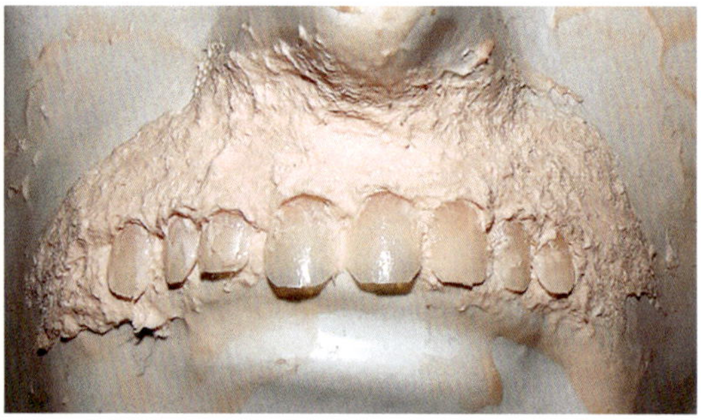

FIGURE 23.3 Step 4

Credit: Christopher Payne

STEP 5

Repeat the previous steps for the lower teeth.

STEP 6

Glue the two prosthetics to your upper and lower lips using spirit gum. Trim the edges with a sharp pair of scissors if you need to; they'll be covered up, so it's okay if the edges are thick.

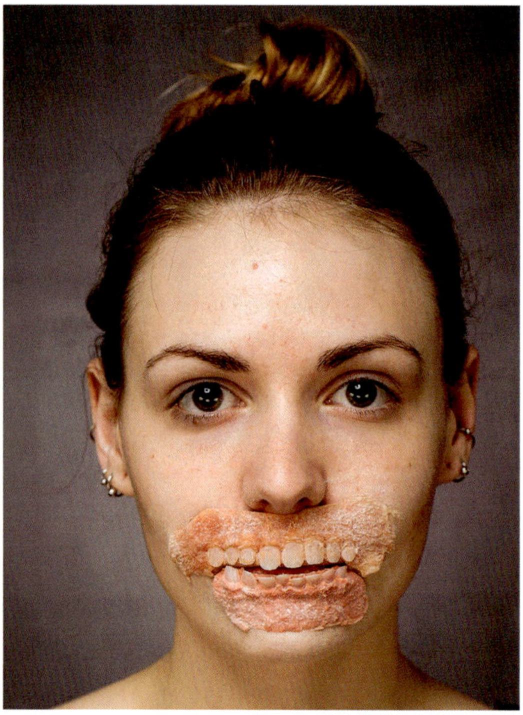

FIGURE 23.4 Step 6

STEP 7

Build up the interior of the sliced grin with latex and cotton. It should have a raw hamburger sort of texture. The exact size and shape of the grin is up to you.

STEP 8

Build up the sliced grin onto your face using nose putty, extending it a bit past the edges of the

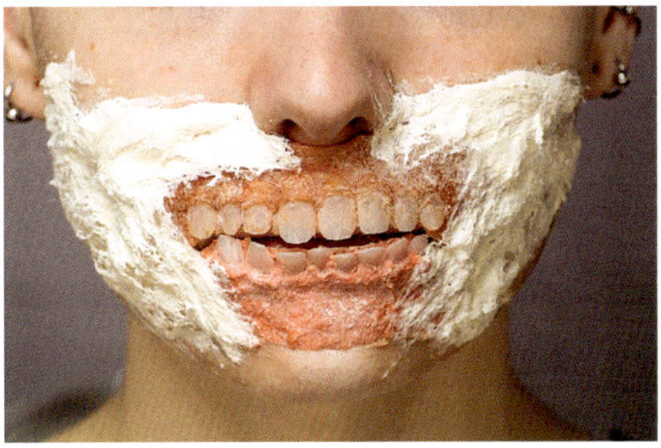

FIGURE 23.5 Step 7

cotton. The more torn and ragged you can make it look, the better.

Blend the outer edges into your skin as smoothly as you can. Because you're working on the more movable part of your cheek, it may be hard to get it perfectly smooth, but you can use clown makeup and blood to hide any funky spots.

STEP 9

Stipple a thin layer of liquid latex over the nose putty to seal it. Powder the latex when it's dry.

STEP 10

Use RMG to paint the interior of the grin a bloody, meaty red. Irregularly mottling in a few different shades will make the wound look more gruesome.

STEP 11

Build up nose putty around your eyes to make them look like empty sockets, creating the illusion that your eyes have been ripped out. Seal the wax with latex and color the interior with the same meaty reds as the mouth.

FIGURE 23.6 Step 8

STEP 12

Apply a coat of white makeup to your face, using white RMG over the latex. Powder it heavily, then add the rest of your clown makeup. You can find lots of examples online if you need some inspiration, but the details are up to you. In this case, I wanted the clown makeup to look smeary and decaying, as if she had been wearing it for a long time.

STEP 13

Tease out your hair to get it really frizzy and then use some spray-in color. If you want, you can use a wig instead.

STEP 14

Finish the makeup by filling in the eye sockets with black makeup and adding fake blood. The amount of blood is up to you, but sometimes strategically placed drips can be scarier than drenching your face. It lets you see the clown beneath.

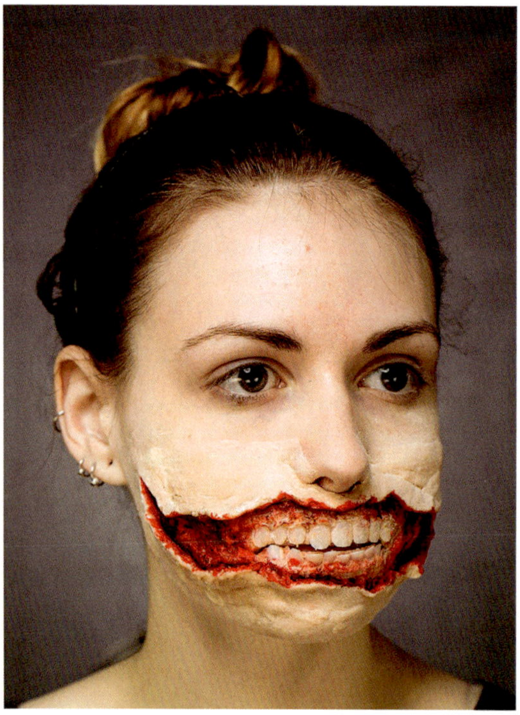

FIGURE 23.7 Step 10

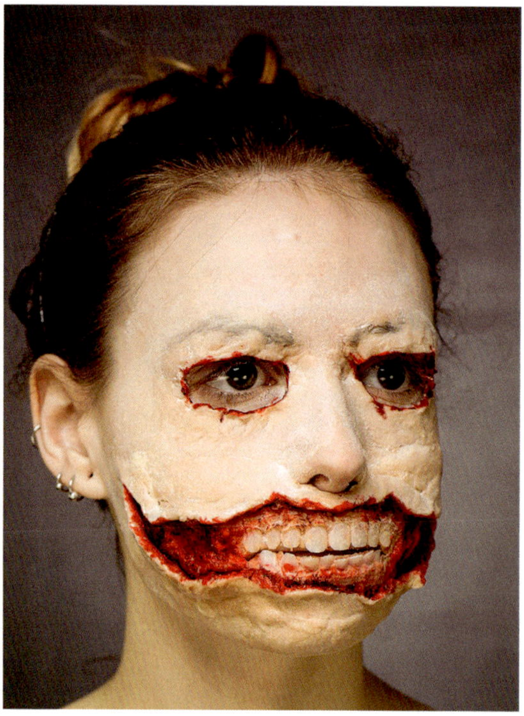

FIGURE 23.8 Step 11

FIGURE 23.9 Step 12

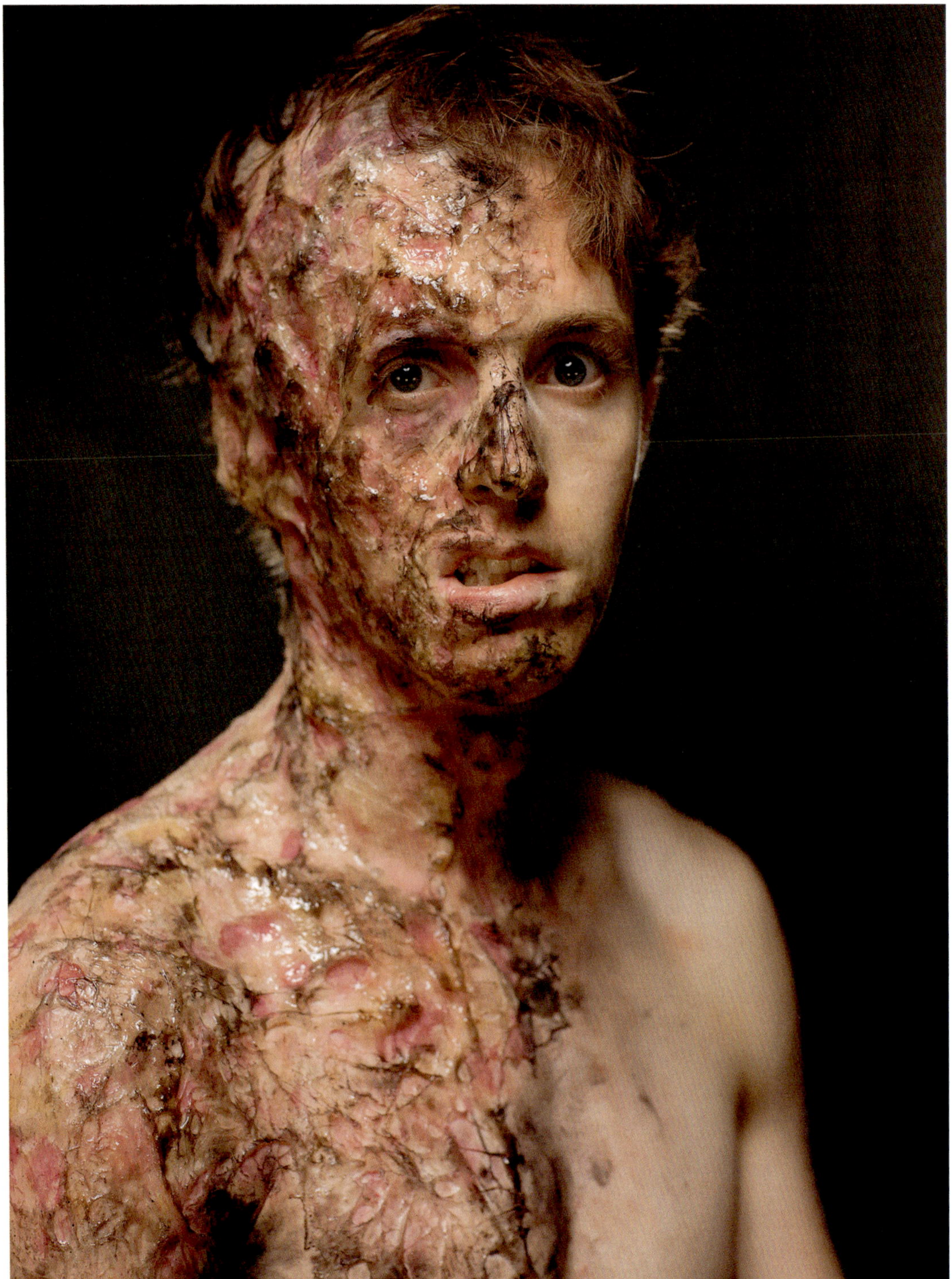

CHAPTER 24

SEVERE BURN

The **Basic Burn** was a fairly simple method for creating a burn injury, but the time has come to create a more advanced (and much gorier) option. You've already used gelatin to create boils, and I briefly mentioned using it for burn scars in the **Skin Texture** chapter. Now you'll use it to produce a **Severe Burn** makeup.

You can use gelatin in your hair without worrying about it getting stuck. If you have longer hair, it helps to either pin it in place first with bobby pins or slick it down with hair gel so you have a flat surface to work on (let the gel dry before you begin the makeup). Using a bald cap for full-head burns will make cleanup a lot easier.

STEP 1

Cut a few strips of flesh-colored tulle or silk. These strips should be about a ½-inch wide and 2 inches long. The more delicate the fabric, the more easily it will disappear into your skin.

STEP 2

Glue the end of a strip to your upper lip, then carefully pull it up and glue the other end to your cheek to pull your lip open into a grimace. Repeat this technique on the lower lip.

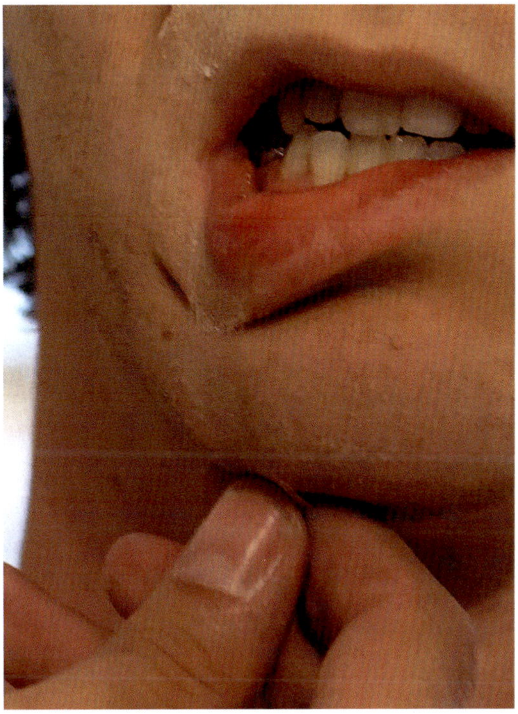

FIGURE 24.1 Step 2

STEP 3

Glue the back of your ear to the skin behind it to flatten it against your head as much as possible.

STEP 4

Mix one tablespoon of unflavored gelatin powder with one tablespoon of hot water in a small cup. As with the plague boils, you can also add a quarter-teaspoon of glycerin to help prevent the gelatin from drying out. This isn't required, but it will help your makeup last longer.

Use a craft stick to mix the water and powder together. Keep stirring the mixture until it begins to cool.

> **Professional Tip:** *Test the temperature of the gelatin on the inside of your wrist. If it's okay on your wrist, it should be okay on your face. Better to have some of the gelatin cool in the cup than to get burned for real!*

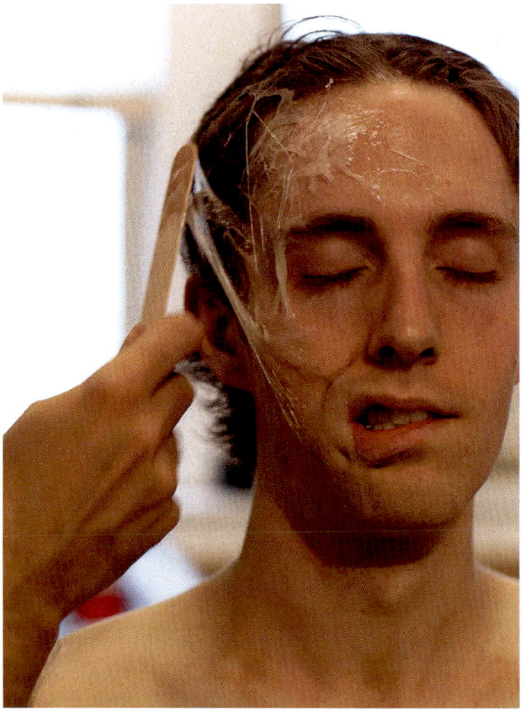

FIGURE 24.2 Step 5 in progress

STEP 5

Spread the gelatin onto a section of your face. Don't worry about covering the whole thing; you will create this makeup using several overlapping batches.

Tap the flat side of your craft stick against the gelatin as it starts to cool, which will pull up strings that you can goop back and forth to get some pretty cool texture. When you're happy with that section, let the gelatin finish cooling.

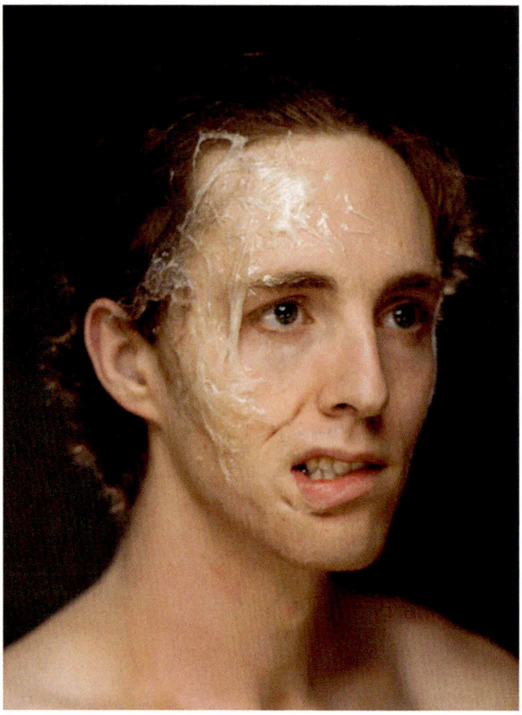

FIGURE 24.3 Step 5 complete

STEP 6

Apply more gelatin to your face, building up the burn gradually section by section. You can extend the gelatin into your hair to make it look like it's been burned away. Your eyebrows can get covered too, but stay away from your eyelashes.

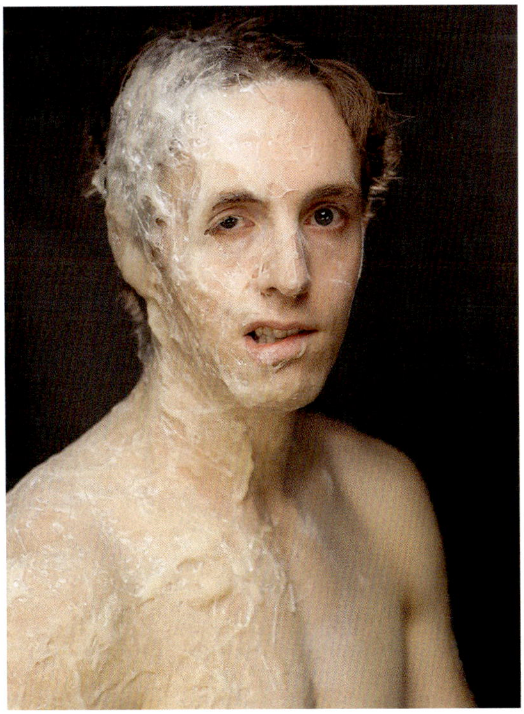

FIGURE 24.4 Step 6

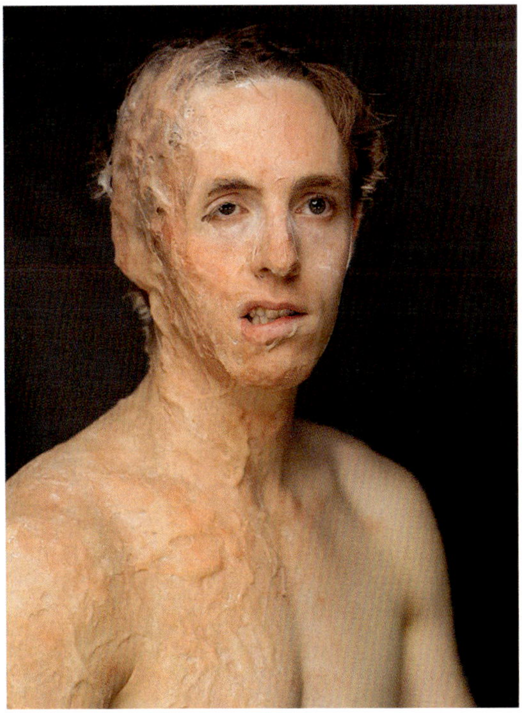

FIGURE 24.5 Step 8

They could get pulled out, and that's way too close to your eyeball to be applying hot gelatin anyway.

STEP 7

Powder the burn when you're done building it up to eliminate the natural stickiness of the gelatin.

STEP 8

Apply sunburn-red makeup over the entire burn, extending it past the edge so it blends into your skin. You can mix the cream makeup with a little rubbing alcohol to create a thin wash of color. As the gelatin has a sort of nasty flesh color already, let some of that show through.

Author's Note: *For a healed burn scar, you can stop here. The following steps will turn the makeup into a fresh, raw burn.*

STEP 9

Shadow the deeper areas with maroon to sink them in and make them look irritated.

STEP 10

Subtly add some pale-yellow highlights here and there to give the impression of melted fat. Don't go too heavy with the yellow (or too bright) or you'll start to get the dreaded pizza face. This is

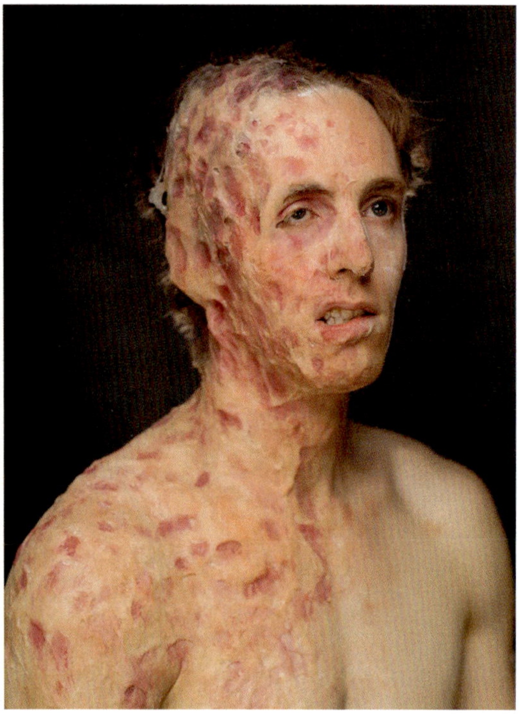

FIGURE 24.6 Step 9

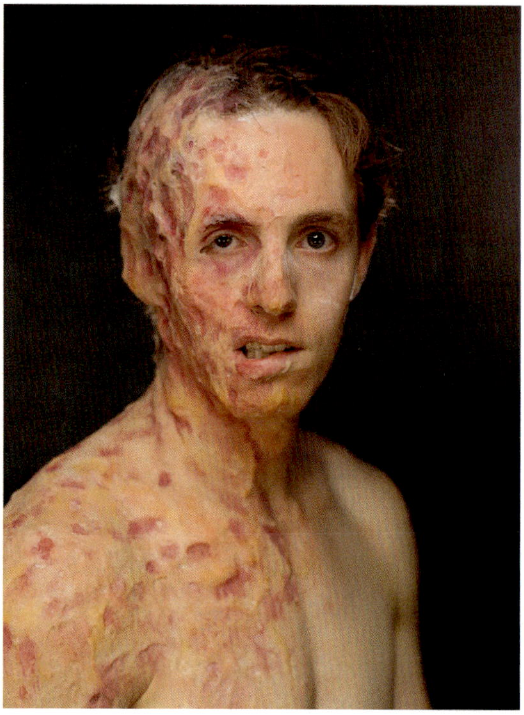

FIGURE 24.7 Step 10

another area where a thin wash of color works better than a heavy coat.

STEP 11

Use the maroon to fill in any exposed skin on your eye as well. Keep this area blotchy so it doesn't look out of place. Powder when you're done.

STEP 12

Lightly add some black to the high points to give the illusion of charred flesh. You can use makeup, black setting powder or even an additive such as crushed Oreos for extra texture (and a chocolatey smell). Subtlety is key here. You took a lot of time doing this makeup, so don't cover the entire thing in a solid layer of black!

STEP 13

Finish the burn with a light coat of KY to give it a shiny, raw appearance. This last step will really make the burn seem nasty. Brush your hair over any hard edges in the gelatin to hide them.

Because gelatin melts in hot water, this makeup is super easy to remove. Just take a hot shower and let it come off on its own! I like to use a drain cover to catch any big chunks, which get thrown away. Anything small enough to slip through the little holes will just dissolve.

CHAPTER 25
GOBLIN

Orcs, imps, gremlins, boogymen. Whatever you call them, **Goblins** are a part of fairy tales and fantasy adventures around the world. They are usually portrayed as creatures of evil – twisted and ugly. That's how I'm going to portray one here, as something that lives underground and hates those who live above.

STEP 1

Apply a bald cap. Beecause Zoë is going to be completely covered with latex, I brought the edge of the cap all the way down below her eyebrows so I wouldn't have to block them out separately.

STEP 2

Apply prosthetic ears, nose and chin. The nose and chin here are reuses of the witch prosthetics that I bought in a costume shop, with the warts removed and trimmed a bit shorter. The ears are the ones I made for the **Making Simple Prosthetics** chapter. If you prefer to use store-bought rubber ears, those work too.

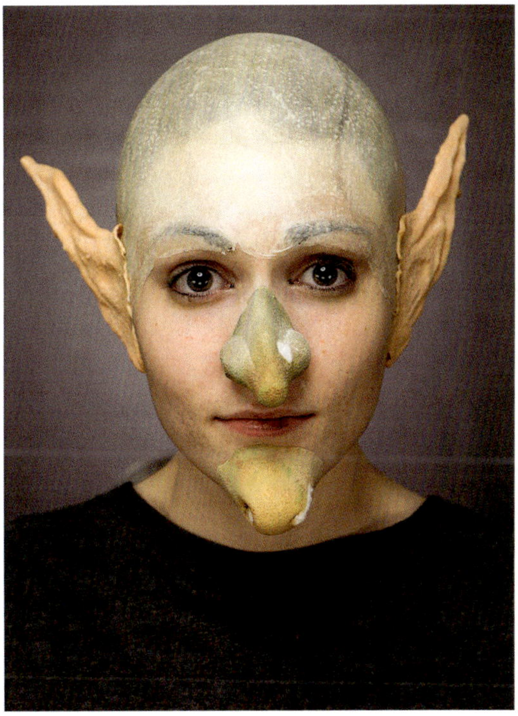

FIGURE 25.1 Steps 1 and 2

STEP 3

Build up your features as described in the **Cotton and Latex** chapter. I wanted the goblin to have a gaunt, skeletal appearance and so I built up the eye sockets, cheekbones, and forehead. I also built up the nasolabial folds to make her look more ferocious.

As always be careful not to get the latex too close to your eyes – the ammonia fumes can irritate them and get stuck in your eyelashes. Having a fan blowing gently across your face as you work can help to dissipate any smell. Eyelash adhesive is an ammonia-free option, but, as it comes in little tubes, the amount used here would get expensive pretty quickly.

STEP 4

Apply a skin of latex and paper towels to your head and neck as described in the **Skin Textures** chapter. You'll want to work in small, overlapping sections, wrinkling the paper towels

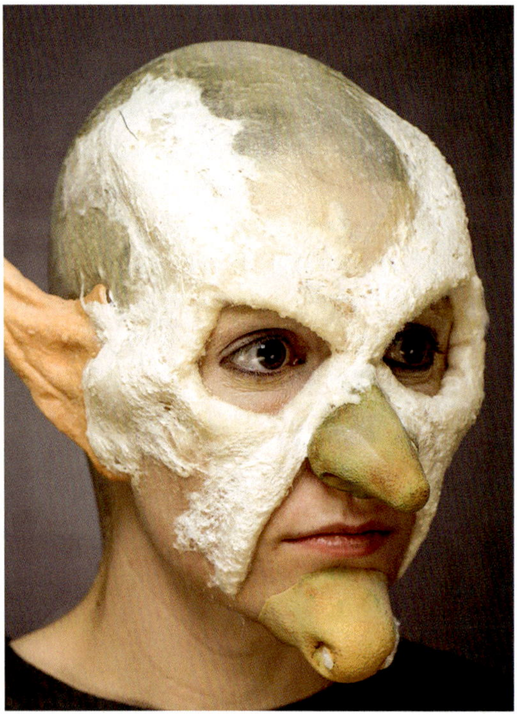

FIGURE 25.2 Step 3

to follow the natural direction of wrinkling for each part of the face. Powder each section once it's done.

Here's my suggestion for the application order:

- Begin with latex and paper towel to your forehead, keeping the wrinkles horizontal. Continue this horizontal wrinkling around the back of the head.
- Now add paper towels around each eye, manipulating the wrinkles to follow the angles of the eye sockets and cheekbones.
- Add paper towel to your nose and chin. Wrinkle direction isn't as important for this step, I made them horizontal to match the forehead.
- Apply a section of paper towel to your upper lip. The wrinkles should be diagonal for this area, radiating away from the center of the mouth and up toward the cheeks. You can do each side as its own section if you want.
- Add paper towels to your cheeks. The wrinkles should travel in roughly an upward diagonal direction from your mouth to your temples. Let the wrinkles of the surrounding sections be a guide.
- Add paper towels above the nasolabial folds, following the downward diagonal direction you established with the cotton.
- Apply paper towels to your neck, keeping the wrinkles horizontal.
- Apply pieces of paper towel over the ears. Direction doesn't matter here; the goal is just to give the ears the same texture as the rest of the face.

I used pictures of elderly people with really weathered faces as reference for the wrinkle direction, which helped a lot. I know I've said it

FIGURE 25.3 Step 4 (front view)

FIGURE 25.4 Step 4 (side view)

before, but reference is your best friend when doing makeup!

STEP 5

Mottle a pale, sickly RMG foundation over your entire head and neck. Keep the texture irregular; nothing about this character should be smooth and pretty. As always, don't forget to powder the RMG.

> **Professional Tip:** *When working with latex and/or makeup on a scale as large as this, it's often easier to use cheap, disposable chip brushes (like you'd use to paint a wall) rather than sponges. Chip brushes are awful if you want a perfectly smooth finish, but, for something with this much texture, they're great.*

STEP 6

Add shadows using dark-brown colors. Because of all the texture, I decided to thin the shadow makeup with rubbing alcohol and spatter it on with a chip brush (outlined in the **Skin Textures** chapter) rather than try to brush or sponge it in place. The only exceptions to this are the lips and the lines inside the ears and along the nasolabial folds – I used a brush for those.

STEP 7

Hand lay some thin, scraggly hair to finish the makeup. You can also leave it bald if you prefer – I think it kind of makes her look like an old, decrepit vampire like in the film Nosferatu.

Finish the character with some nasty teeth, which you can make following the instructions in the **Teeth** chapter.

FIGURE 25.5 Step 5

FIGURE 25.6 Step 6

Back when I was removing the Witch makeup, Zoë and I started goofing around with the Goblin ears (see Figure 25.7).

This photo is fun, but it also illustrates a point when it comes to character design. On the Goblin, the ears angle upwards, which suggests strength and aggressiveness. I also angled the eye sockets upward for the same reason, to create the appearance of an angry snarl.

In Figure 25.7, they droop down, which suggests weakness and sadness. Even without Zoë's sad expression, she would look meeker and elicit pity. It's a subtle trick you can incorporate into your makeups to help define the character.

FIGURE 25.7

CHAPTER 26
THE CREATURE

The Creature pays homage to the classic monsters of the early days of cinema, where creepy crawlers always seemed to be shambling through jungles or swimming up from the deep. A lot of the inspiration for this character comes from the angler fish, which is (in my opinion) one of the scariest animals out there. Seriously, go look it up. Nightmare fuel.

FIGURE 26.1 Step 1: teeth drying

STEP 1

I chose to make the jaws and teeth in advance using cotton and latex on a generic plastic mask. The lower jaw should go down along your chin, and the upper goes over the bridge of your nose.

The teeth are made of paper clay, which I set on a piece of 4-inch PVC pipe so they would dry with a curved shape. You can always build up the jaws on your face, but the advantage to making them in advance was that I could glue the teeth in place with super glue for a really secure fit.

This should be obvious, but *do not* use super glue anywhere near your actual face.

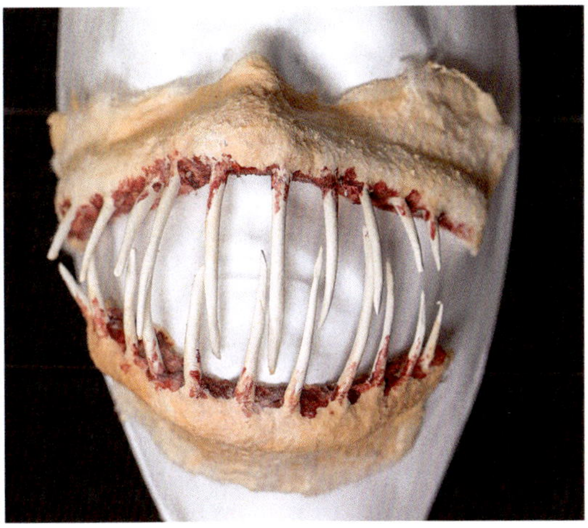

FIGURE 26.2 Step 1: Finished jaws

STEP 2

I also made the eyes in advance. I cut a ping pong ball in half with a pair of cuticle scissors and then trimmed the edges to fit the curvature of Jessica's face. You can either cut the pupil out or melt it into the plastic with a soldering iron. Give the cut/melted edges a good sanding to remove any sharp edges. I based the shape here on the eyes of a gecko.

I didn't add any more detail to the eyes until I was doing the makeup; in hindsight, it would have been easier to paint them in advance, so that's what I'm going to recommend. Use acrylic or spray paint and then pull some fluff from red yarn and glue it in place in the corners for bloodshot veins. Seal the finished eyes with clear enamel spray for a nice shine.

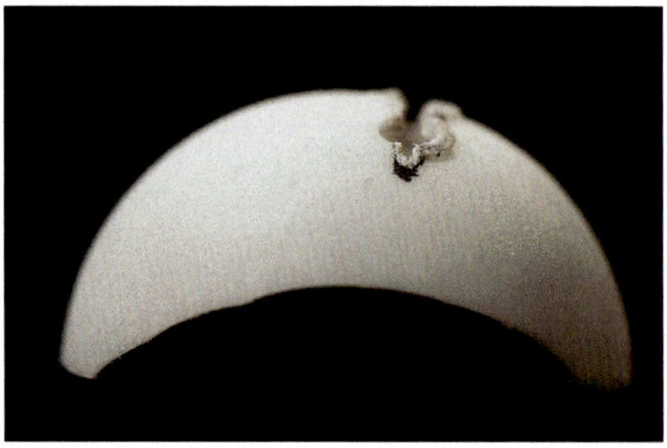

FIGURE 26.3 Step 2 (before sanding)

STEP 3

Apply a bald cap, covering your eyebrows and ears.

STEP 4

Apply black makeup to the lower part of your face and then glue the jaws in place. Use more cotton and latex to connect the corners of the upper and lower jaws, completing the mouth.

STEP 5

Secure the eyes in place with nose putty. You don't need to worry about it looking pretty; most of it will be covered up in the next step. This will be your only chance to adjust the placement, so make sure you're happy with them before moving on.

STEP 6

Use cotton and latex to create the eyelid area. You can use a popsicle stick to sculpt the wet latex as needed. I modeled the eyelids in a downward-sweeping direction, following the shape of the mouth, to make this creature look angry and mean.

STEP 7

Cut strips of 1-inch sheet foam and then bevel the edges to create long triangular shapes. Stick these in place with liquid latex to form ridges along your face.

I found it easiest to apply latex to the back of the foam and the bald cap, let them dry and then press them together. The fresh latex surfaces will naturally stick together. If you try to stick the foam to wet latex it will want to pop loose again.

STEP 8

Apply a skin of latex and paper towels over the foam and any exposed skin. I also used cotton and latex to build up the neck structure.

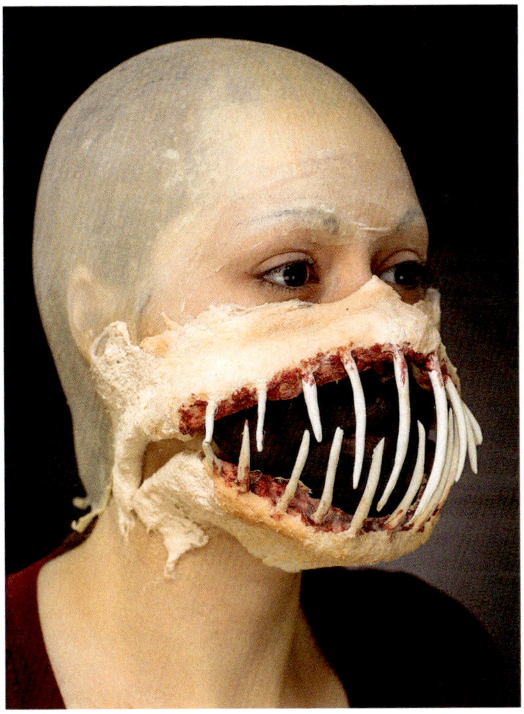

FIGURE 26.4 Step 4

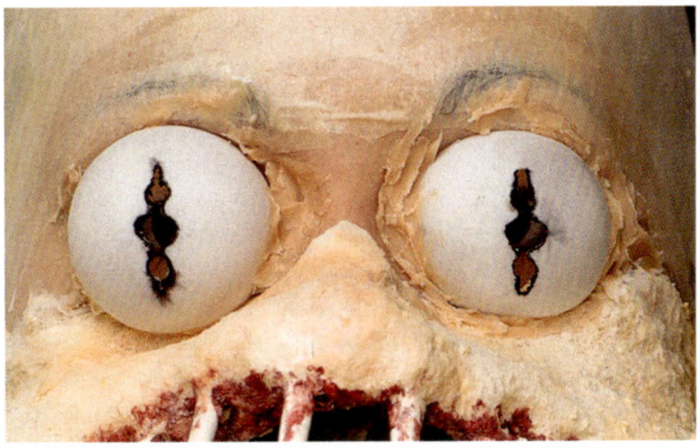

FIGURE 26.5 Step 5

FIGURE 26.6 Step 6

STEP 9

Now it's time to begin adding scale texture, using the latex and additives technique covered in the **Skin Textures** chapter. For the smaller scales I used liquid latex and puffed rice cereal; the larger scales are a mixture of dried lima and kidney beans. Split the beans in half so you have a nice flat surface to stick down.

This is a pretty messy step (especially the cereal), and it's a good idea to lay down a tarp or work somewhere you can sweep up later. Sticking all of those beans by hand also took a *long* time. In hindsight, the application would have gone faster if I had glued the beans to pieces of paper towel in advance. That way I could have applied large sections of scales instead of gluing them on one by one. Live and learn.

STEP 10

Apply a pale green RMG to your entire head, making sure to work it in between the scales (mixing it with a little alcohol helps get it in the deep parts). Then, stipple a darker green makeup over the entire surface with a coarse stipple sponge or sea sponge to add a little texture.

FIGURE 26.7 Step 7

FIGURE 26.8 Step 8

FIGURE 26.9 Step 9: Small scales

FIGURE 26.10 Step 9: Medium and large scales

FIGURE 26.11 Step 10

FIGURE 26.12 Step 11

FIGURE 26.13 Step 12

STEP 11

Use the darker green for a shadow color and mustard yellow for highlights.

STEP 12

Add additional colors and patterns however you want. Once again, look to pictures of real animals for inspiration. I've collected an entire shelf of books with animals from the desert, from the ocean, from the rainforest. So many cool color patterns just begging to be used!

FIGURE 26.14 Step 13

STEP 13

If you didn't pre-paint the eyes, do that now. With them in place using paint isn't an option, but you can use cream makeup well enough, and the yarn fluff veins can be glued in place with spirit gum. Finally, apply baby oil or KY to the entire makeup for a slimy shine.

I only did the head and neck for this book, but there's no reason why you can't bring the scales as far down your body as you want. In fact, incorporating more of the body is exactly what the next makeup is all about.

CHAPTER 27
ADVANCED ZOMBIE

So far nearly all of the makeups in this book have been just on your head and neck. With the **Advanced Zombie**, we're going bigger: a makeup that covers large areas of your chest as well.

Even though I applied this makeup on a man, there's no reason women can't do it too. The only difference is that a woman may need to wrap her chest in a disposable elastic bandage first to get as flat a surface as possible for the ribs. I had Misael shave his chest before this makeup; otherwise, he would have gotten a free waxing when the latex came off.

STEP 1

Once again there were elements of this makeup that I chose to fabricate in advance to shorten the already hefty application time. I made upper and lower teeth the same way I did for **Giggles**, only this time I sculpted the individual teeth in paper clay rather than using press-on nails. I glued a bit of lace to each tooth once it was dry and then built up the gums with cotton and latex the same way as before.

I also built up the ribcage using latex and cotton batting. For better accuracy, I printed a life-size picture of a ribcage I found online, which I split across four sheets of paper taped together. After covering the paper with cling wrap, I had a perfect outline to follow.

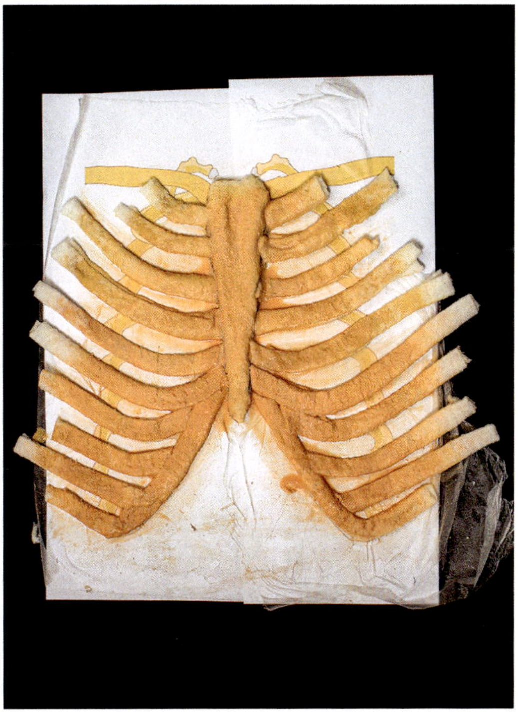

FIGURE 27.1 The ribcage made in advance

STEP 2

Apply a bald cap, leaving the ears exposed (or, if you prefer, cover one ear and build up a chewed-off stump with cotton and latex).

STEP 3

Apply tissue and latex texture to your neck. You're adding this texture first because getting that neck stretch when the whole torso is covered in latex could get tight and uncomfortable around the upper chest.

STEP 4

Glue the ribcage to your chest, lining it up as closely as you can with your own ribs. You can use spirit gum for this or just use liquid latex as it's all going to be sealed in place in the next step.

STEP 5

Go over your entire neck, chest and stomach with a layer of latex and paper towels. You'll want to work the paper towels down into the gaps between the ribs to make the skin look shrunken and withered.

At this point, women may want to go back in with craft foam or cotton and latex to make some mummified, rotting breasts. If you do, be sure to skin them with latex and paper towels so the entire surface has the same texture.

STEP 6

Glue the teeth in place. At this point I also covered Misael's eyebrows with scraps cut out of the bald cap to protect them from the latex to come (or block them with wax to protect them).

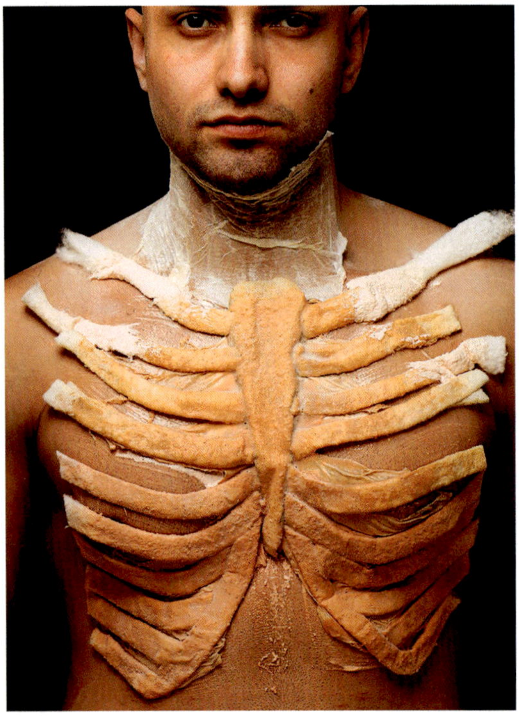

FIGURE 27.2 Step 4

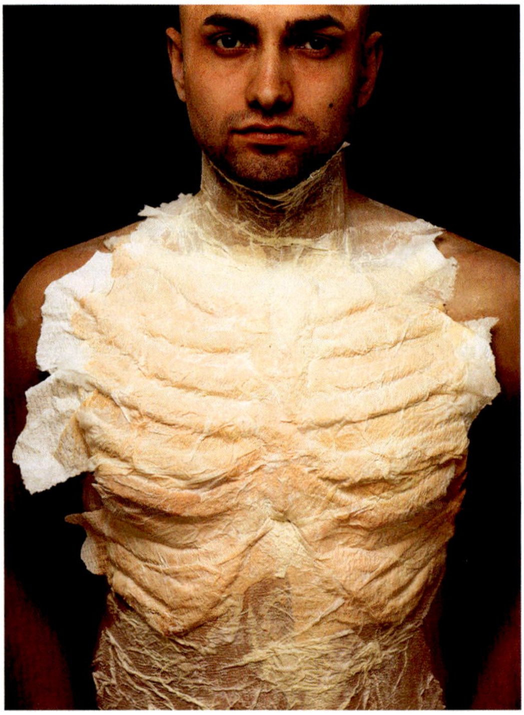

FIGURE 27.3 Step 5

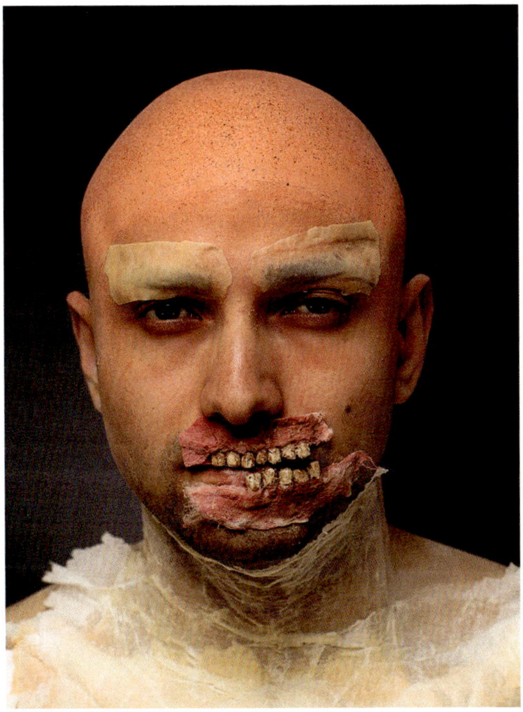

FIGURE 27.4 Step 6

FIGURE 27.5 Step 7

If you prefer, you could also just bring the bald cap down under your eyebrows as I've done a few times previously.

STEP 7

Build up some lip structure using cotton and latex, leaving the area around the teeth looking torn away.

STEP 8

Build up the rest of the structure on your head and neck, really emphasizing the bone structure to make your face appear sunken in. As with previous makeups, look at pictures of skulls (or a plastic model if you have one) to get the forms right.

Once you have the anatomy built up, go in with more latex and cotton to add a few large wounds.

STEP 9

Cover the entire surface with latex and paper towels so that it matches your chest.

Author's Note: *There's no reason why you can't do your face first and your chest second if you'd prefer; this is just the order I chose to work in. You're the artist, make this zombie your own!*

STEP 10

Apply a pale RMG foundation to your entire head, neck and chest. For this I used a pale, sickly flesh tone to begin with and then stippled on lighter and darker flesh colors to get a mottled surface. I used a chip brush for this; a sea sponge will offer a bolder texture if that's what you want.

STEP 11

Use highlight and shadow to further sculpt your zombie's features. Be sure to keep everything mottled and irregular!

STEP 12

Fill in your wounds with a reddish-brown color to simulate coagulated blood. You could also use some blood paste as well. Any portions of exposed skull should be painted ivory.

STEP 13

At this stage I was almost done, but I decided the skin was still looking a bit too smooth, so I increased the intensity of the mottling (should have used that sea sponge). The skin tone doesn't have to be done in multiple steps like this; it's just how this makeup evolved.

I also painted the remaining portions of the lips a more realistic color.

STEP 14

Lay on some scraggly hair if you want, or just leave your zombie bald. I always feel that a bit of hair takes the whole character to the next level, but that's just me. Same thing with the eyebrows. I like adding eyebrows to a character like this, but there is no right or wrong. If you prefer a hairless zombie, go for it!

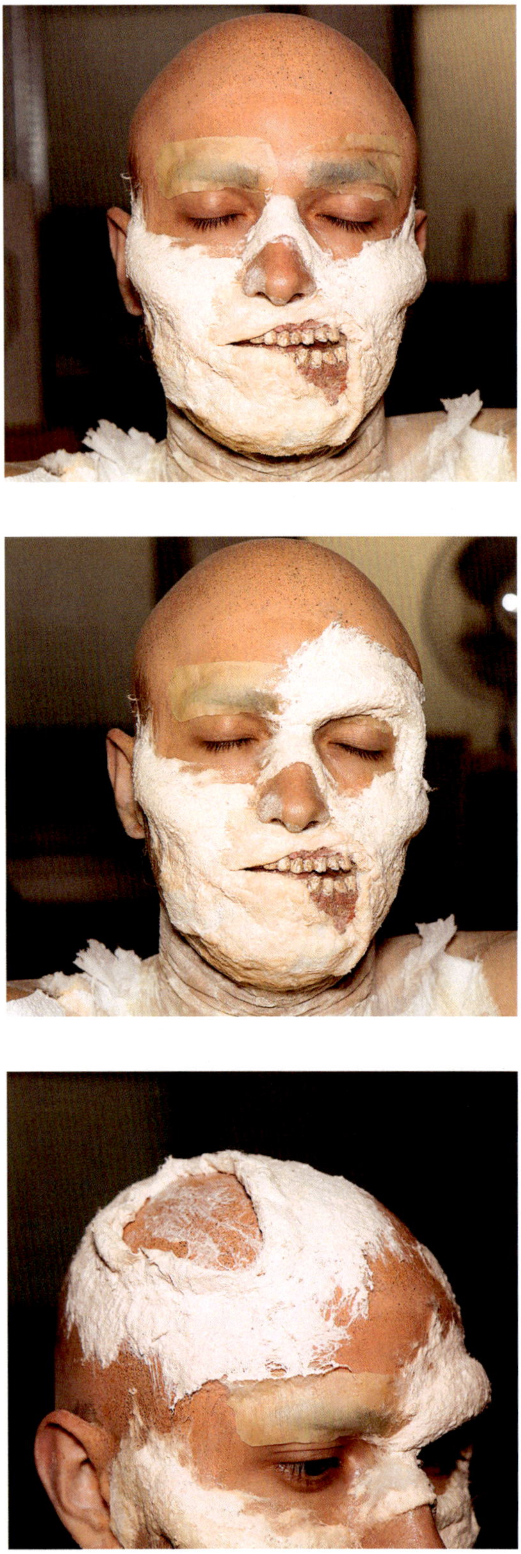

FIGURE 27.6–27.8 Step 8 in progress

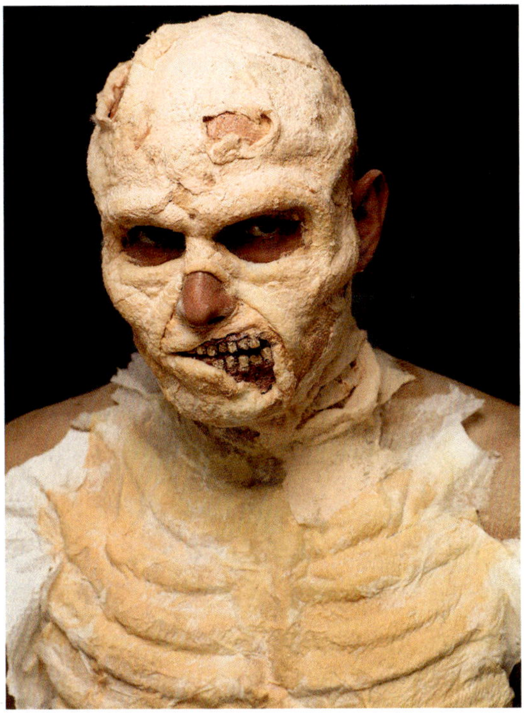

FIGURE 27.9 Step 8 completed

FIGURE 27.10 Step 10

FIGURE 27.11 Step 11

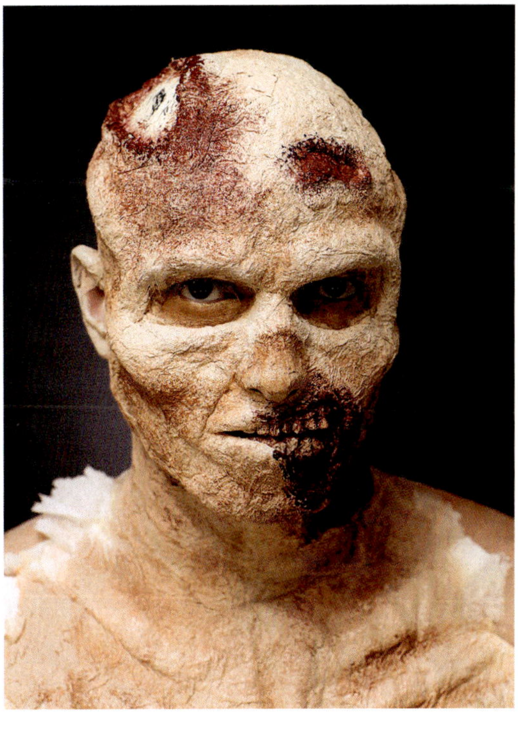

FIGURE 27.12 Step 12

STEP 15

Last, but not least, dress up in some appropriate clothing. Sometimes I like to smear some bright fake blood on the mouth area: it makes it look like you've just fed and contrasts nicely with your own dry, crusty blood.

One of the fun things about a heavy latex and paper towel makeup like this (as you may have discovered with a few of the previous ones) is that, if you're careful, you can remove the entire thing in one piece and either wear it again or display it!

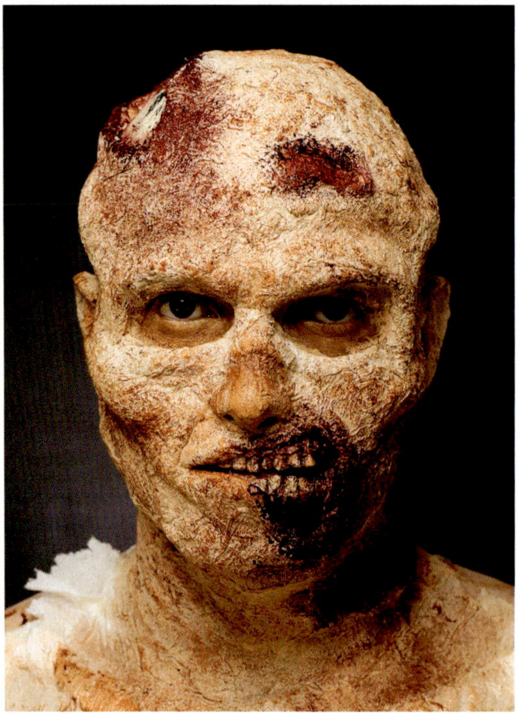

FIGURE 27.13 Step 13

FIGURE 27.14

CHAPTER 28

PIRATE … AGAIN

Congratulations, you've almost made it to the end! Go back and look at photos of your first Pirate makeup. You've come a long way since then! I thought it would be fun to revisit that first makeup with some of the things you've learned over the course of the book. So, let's do the **Pirate … again**.

STEP 1

Apply a mottled foundation a couple of shades darker than your own, followed by a sunburn color. Remember to focus that second layer on the areas of your face that get the most sun (forehead, nose, cheekbones, chin).

STEP 2

Add some cuts and scars using any of the techniques you learned in this book. I did some nasty rigid collodion scars and a smaller keloid one with eyelash adhesive.

STEP 3

Apply more rigid collodion randomly on your cheeks, forehead and neck to create a really pockmarked skin texture.

STEP 4

Lay on a crepe wool goatee. The placement of my cheek scar meant I had to leave a gap in Jake's goatee, which just made it more interesting.

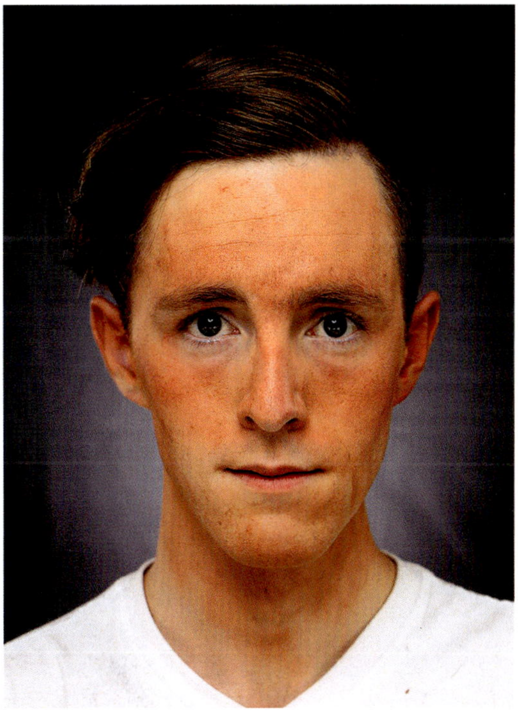

FIGURE 28.1 Step 1

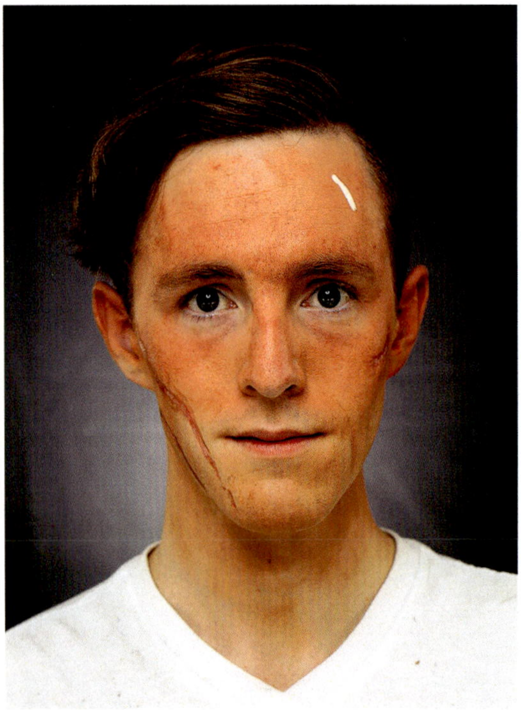

FIGURE 28.2 Step 2

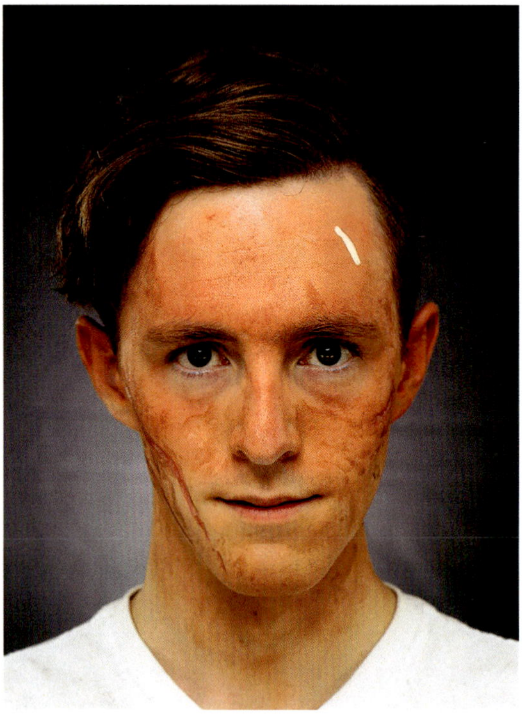

FIGURE 28.3 Step 3

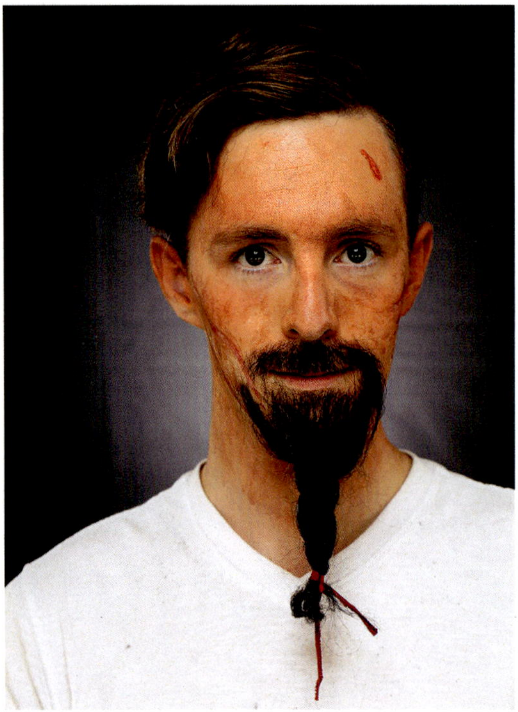

FIGURE 28.4 Step 4

STEP 5

Apply chopped hair stubble to your cheeks and neck. The length and thickness are completely up to you.

Darken your eyebrows with a makeup pencil if you need to, or go really big with more crepe wool.

STEP 6

Use brown, yellow and black tooth enamel to create some disgusting rotting teeth. As always, finish off the character with costume and a wig.

Think about techniques you've learned that you can adapt to this character. For example, you could pull a sock over your hand, create a cotton and latex stump on it and give people a nasty show when you pull off your hook!

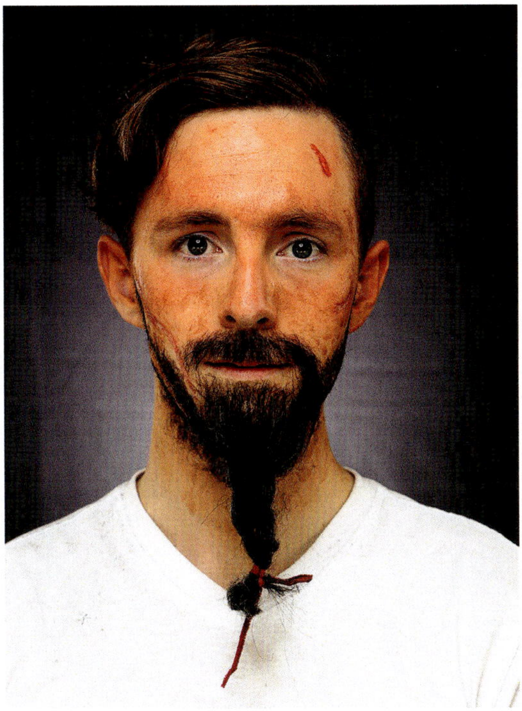

FIGURE 28.5 Step 5

Or you could apply a bald cap and draw tattoos with makeup pencils for a fearsome warrior pirate!

Combine this with a zombie makeup for an undead pirate? Why not? Disney may have done it first, but it's still a cool look (plus, don't forget what I said about guyliner).

That's the amazing thing about special effects makeup. Once you've learned a variety of tricks and techniques, you can combine them in an infinite number of ways. You're only limited by your imagination, so get out there and make some monsters!

APPENDIX 1

SKINCARE AND SANITATION

If this is so important, why is it at the end? Mostly because I didn't want to bog you down with a lot of non-monster stuff at the very beginning. But it is important, so hopefully you skipped ahead like I suggested at the end of that first Pirate makeup.

As a professional makeup artist, taking care of my actor's skin (and health in general) is priority #1. Knowing a thing or two about skincare and proper sanitation falls into that. You don't have to be a licensed esthetician or anything, but having a little knowledge under your belt can help to keep everyone safe.

SKINCARE

There's no getting around the fact that special effects makeup can be rough on your skin; even heavy paint-only makeups such as **Vampire** or **Ghost** can be tough if you're doing several each day. The first step is taking care of your skin in general, not just when you're about to do a makeup. Wearing sunscreen when you're outside, moisturizing every day and drinking plenty of water all contribute to healthy skin. Eating right, getting enough sleep, all that. I'm not saying you need to adopt a radical lifestyle change just to turn yourself into the occasional monster, but these little things really do add up in the long run (especially when you pass the age of 30 or so).

But let's talk specific skincare for makeup. The first step is to clean and assess your skin before you start. For cleaning, I like to first wash my face with a facial cleanser, then do a light wipe-down with either an astringent or toner on a cotton ball. This will help to remove any extra oils and any dirt that the wash may have missed. Astringents often contain alcohol, so they can be a little rougher on sensitive skin, but they also tend to be cheaper and cut through dirt and oil faster.

Once the skin is clean, I apply a little moisturizer and give it a couple of minutes to settle in. There are different moisturizers designed for the three main kinds of skin: oily, dry and combination (typically, oily in the center but dry around the edges). Picking the right one will help you get the most out of it. You don't need the most expensive moisturizer on the planet, but it's worth investing in something a little nicer than the stuff from the discount bin.

From time to time we all have breakouts, it's a part of life. Minor open sores (a popped pimple, etc.) can be covered with a little liquid bandage or you can simply avoid doing makeup on that area. If it's a bad breakout, you should think about waiting until it clears up. Caking a bunch of product over skin that's already irritated is just going to make things worse. Obviously, if you have open cuts, fresh scrapes, massive burns or full-face transplants, you should wait until they heal before doing makeup.

Good skincare continues after the makeup is over as well. The first step is to take your time removing any prosthetics, glues, latex, basically whatever you've stuck to your face. Using the proper remover and going slowly is key; if you just rip stuff off, your skin *will* suffer for it. Even those things that are peeled off (like latex and tissue) can be done properly, taking your time, instead of yanking it off like a Band-Aid.

The next big thing is to wash your face! This seems basic, but I've seen a lot of people do a quick wipe-down with a baby wipe and consider the job done (or even go to sleep with their makeup on because they just got home from a party and are tired). Big. Mistake. Baby wipes don't catch everything, and any makeup left on overnight is just a breakout waiting to happen.

I like to start my cleanup with a hot towel. Roll up a wet washcloth, wring out the excess water and microwave it for about 45 seconds. When it's cooled enough, hold it against your face for a bit to let the heat work its magic and then gently use it to clean your face. That alone will get a lot of the makeup off, plus it helps to loosen the hold of glues and latex so they come off more easily. Next, do a proper cleanse with the same facial cleanser you started with and, finally, moisturize again to rehydrate your skin.

Another way to keep your skin healthy is to not abuse it with intense makeup every single day. Ask any theater actor who has to wear heavy greasepaint for two performances a day – it gets rough after a while. Films that have actors in heavy prosthetics will often schedule days off for them so their skin can take a break to heal every few days. That's also where the lifestyle choices (sunscreen, drinking plenty of water and the rest) come in. The healthier your skin is going in, the better off it will be coming out.

One last thing to consider is allergies. Any makeup you'll buy from a legitimate manufacturer is hypoallergenic, meaning it's designed to be safe on your skin. Still, weird things happen. If something you're using is causing you to break out, stop using it! Chances are the biggest culprit is going to be latex. Around 5% (give or take) of the population has some form of latex allergy, meaning that using liquid latex is a no-no. If you're not sure, try applying a drip to the inside of your wrist. If you're fine after a few hours, great. If you have an allergy, your skin will get red and itchy. If that's the case, skip the makeups in this book that use latex (or do them on someone else while wearing latex-free gloves).

SANITATION

Whether you're doing makeup on yourself or on your friends, it's a good idea to practice proper sanitation techniques. Just because you're working on yourself today doesn't mean you won't use those brushes and products on someone else tomorrow.

The most important thing when it comes to your product is to never work directly out of the container if you can avoid it. Dipping into the same container for several people can spread germs and is called cross-contamination. That's where a palette comes in handy. You can use anything so long as it's non-porous. A plastic palette from an art store, a large shower tile from a hardware store, whatever you want. In a pinch, I've even used plastic party plates. When using cream makeups, putty, gel blood, etc., scoop out a little bit onto the palette to work with using a spatula. That way you won't double dip into the makeup container, risking contaminating the whole thing from your used brushes.

Anything that pours (blood, liquid latex, etc.) should be decanted into a smaller container that you can work out of for the same reason. Those little deli cups that restaurants use to serve to-go salsas and sauces work great. You can also get metal cups from restaurant supply stores, which helps to cut down on the amount of trash you create. I use both: disposable cups for glues and things that would be really hard to clean out, and metal cups for everything else. Make sure you wash those metal cups well between makeups.

Some kinds of makeup, such as pancakes and pressed powders, must be used by dipping into the container again and again. There's no real way around it. In the case of water-activated products such as pancake makeup, *never* close it up while it's still wet. You'll have literally created a petri dish and a germ farm. Instead, every time you're done using these products, let them dry, then spray the surface with rubbing alcohol and wipe the surface with a clean tissue. This will remove the top layer (and any germs with it). Just to be safe, spray it a second time and let it dry.

Makeup pencils should be sharpened after use, which removes the contaminated surface layer. Use a makeup pencil sharpener, not just something out of your desk. The former is designed to work with softer makeup pencils; the latter is not. After sharpening, give your pencils a spray with alcohol to finish the job.

Finally, there's a small range of products that you apply directly from the container onto the skin, such as latex eyelash adhesive when creating raised scars. In those cases, every single person you work on (including you) should have their own that is only for that person. There's no chance of cross-contamination if nobody else will ever use it. Write the person's name on the container in permanent marker.

Keeping your brushes clean is also super important. A lot of people think that if they're only doing makeup on themselves, it's not as big a deal. That's just not true (and kind of gross). You want to clean them with either brush cleaner or strong alcohol, both available at drugstores (alcohol is good for brushes with synthetic fibers, but can be rough on natural fiber brushes). The two main ways to clean your brushes are either to spray them with cleaner and then wipe them on a paper towel until no more product comes off, or to dip just the bristles into a jar of cleaner and wipe them the same way. While you're at it, giving the handle a wipe down is a good idea too. Any spatulas and other tools should also be cleaned with alcohol before being put away. If you accidentally drop a brush or tool while you're working, it's done. Set it aside until you can clean it properly. There's no 5-second rule in this business.

You have a lot of disposable products available to you, and they should be treated as just that: disposable. Never be tempted to reuse sponges, cotton swabs or anything else designed to be used once and discarded. Even for products that come with their own applicator (such as mascara and spirit gum), you should use a disposable applicator and then throw it away to avoid any possible cross-contamination. If you do use the applicator that comes with it, that whole bottle belongs to your model now. Never, ever use it on someone else. I know it can be a pain having to buy this disposable stuff over and over, but the alternative just isn't worth it (and, again, *gross*).

Technically, cloth powder puffs are considered disposable, but that's one area where I feel you can cheat. You can get a few uses out of each one, provided that you wash it each time (I toss mine in the laundry). Even doing this, however, after a few uses it's time to say goodbye.

Personal hygiene is also very important as a makeup artist. Beyond the basics such as brushing your teeth and putting on deodorant (remember, you're going to be working inches from someone's face), it's vital to keep your hands as clean as your tools. Wash them before you start, and don't touch your face while you're working. I keep a bottle of hand sanitizer at my makeup station just in case I forget and I make sure the actor can see me using it.

If you or your model is feeling sick, don't do the makeup. Just don't. I shouldn't have to say that, but even in the professional world I've seen both makeup artists and actors show up for work obviously sick. I understand that people have to eat, but I don't want to catch anything from you, and you don't want to catch anything from me. It's common sense.

Everything I've talked about here especially applies if you're working on several people in a row. When you're done with the first person, the brushes you used get set aside, and you break out clean ones for the next person. Throw away your disposables and get new ones ready. Clean your palette and spatulas and sanitize any makeup product that needs it. Wash your hands before starting on the next person.

All of this can seem like a lot of work, and it is. But, if you want to be a makeup artist (or even just work on your friends for fun), it's part of the game. Think about it like this: if you just did a makeup on someone, would you be willing to immediately do another on your own face without cleaning things first?

I sure hope not.

APPENDIX 2

GLOSSARY

adhesive Another term for "glue." Adhesives work at a microscopic level and typically need a matching remover to dissolve

astringent A makeup cleanser designed to remove dirt and oils from the skin. Astringents also constrict skin pores

bald cap A thin, prosthetic covering for the head that simulates baldness

base *See* **foundation**

buildup The process of creating a 3D makeup directly on the face instead of in advance. Examples include cotton and latex, gelatin and nose putty

contouring The process of using shadow to make the bone structure more pronounced

crow's feet The common name for the horizontal wrinkles extending from the outside of each eye. They become more pronounced with age

foundation The first layer of makeup applied, often matching the model's skin tone (or the skin tone of a character if different)

hard edge A shadow or highlight with a crisp, defined line for an edge

highlight A lighter, more raised surface. This can be recreated with makeup by using a color brighter than the foundation

hypoallergenic Something that is designed to minimize the chances of an allergic reaction by using no irritating substances

nasolabial folds The diagonal "smile lines" extending from your nostrils down to the sides of your mouth. They become more pronounced with age

opacifier A substance added to a makeup product to make it more opaque

pigment A substance or chemical used to add color to a makeup product

powdering Applying a setting powder to makeup to set the makeup (prevent it from smearing)

prosthetics A premade facial or body feature that is attached to the skin with adhesive.

Examples of prosthetics include character noses, chins and ears

reference Any source of information used as inspiration or example for a makeup. Books, magazines, photographs, drawings and the internet are all reference sources

registration Using a heavy coat of powder to mark the placement of a prosthetic before applying glue

remover A product designed to dissolve and remove either makeup or adhesive

shadow A darker, deeper surface. This can be recreated with makeup by using a color darker than the foundation.

soft edge A shadow or highlight edge that is diffuse, fading away into the surrounding makeup

stippling Applying a makeup product using a dabbing motion, as opposed to brushing. Often used to create textures such as beard stubble, mottled skin, etc.

stretch and stipple A technique of stretching areas of the face in order to create realistic wrinkles using a product such as liquid latex

toner A product similar to astringent but typically made without alcohol

vehicle The main ingredient in a makeup or blood, which facilitates the other ingredients mixed into it

INDEX

Locators in *italics* refer to full-page figures.